PHILIPPINES dos & don'ts

in the Philippines

By
Maida Pineda

Illustrations by
Stephanie Bravo

ISBN 1-84464-004-3

Copyright © 2005 Book Promotion and Service Co., Ltd.

Published in Thailand by
Book Promotion and Service Co., Ltd.
2220/31 Ramkhamhaeng 36/1
Huamark, Bangkok 10240
Thailand
Tel: +66 2 7320243-5
Fax: +66 2 3752669
E-mail: booknet@book.co.th
Distribution:
UK & Ireland: Paths International Ltd.
               P O BOX 4083
               Reading, Berkshire
               RG8 8ZN
               U.K.
               E-mail: pathsmail@aol.com

Rest of the world: Booknet Co., Ltd.
                    1173, 1175, 1177, 1179 Srinakharin Road
                    Suan Luang, Bangkok 10250
                    Thailand
                    Tel: +66 2 3223678
                    Fax: +66 2 7211639
                    E-mail: booknet@book.co.th

Printed and bound in Thailand by
Amarin Printing & Publishing Public Company Limited

All rights reserved. No part of this publication may be reproduced, stored in a retrieval system, or transmitted in any form or by any means, electronic, mechanical, photocopying, recording or otherwise, without the prior permission of the publisher.

dos & don'ts in the PHILIPPINES

page	CONTENTS
1	The Pinoy
25	Religion
33	History of the Filipino People
37	Accommodation
43	Celebrations
53	Cinema
57	Dining Pinoy Style
69	Emergency
73	Fiestas & Festivals
81	Friend's house
89	Funeral & the Wake
93	Holidays
101	Language
107	Mainly for Men
113	Public Places
119	Rentals
125	Restaurants
133	Shopping
137	Superstitious Beliefs & Folk Practices
143	Swimming, Scuba Diving & Snorkelling
149	Touring & Trekking
157	Travelling & Getting Around
171	Visiting the Sick
173	Mainly for Women
177	Zoos, Parks & Museums
179	Zigzags

dos & don'ts **in the PHILIPPINES**

dos & don'ts **in the PHILIPPINES**

THE PINOY

Philippines

Traditional Filipino values

Philippines, Filipinos, Filipinas, . . . not only is it a tongue twister, it's also very confusing for visitors. Before you get mixed up with all the terms, let's clarify the basics. The people from the Philippine islands are called 'Filipinos' in English, 'Pinoys' (as the Filipinos calls themselves in colloquial) and 'Pilipino' in the native language. When indicating a female gender, 'Filipina', 'Pinay', or 'Pilipina' are used.

The country's name, Philippines, is spelled with a p and an h, since it was named after King Philip II of Spain in the 1500's. It can also be spelled Filipinas. Since the national language has no f or h in its alphabet, it is also written as Pilipinas.

While most reside in the archipelago, many Filipinos are scattered throughout the world seeking a better life or working hard to send money home to their families. It's most likely that you've met a Filipino at least once in your life, or even have some Filipino friends. If not, you are sure to make new friends when you visit these 7,107 islands.

Whether you encounter Filipinos in their home country or in a foreign land, their people-oriented nature will surely strike you. You'll soon notice a close bond that connects them. Filipinos automatically consider the effect of their actions and behaviour on the lives of friends and relatives, keeping their best interests in mind.

This interdependence among Filipinos stems from a set of traditional values passed on from generation to generation. The traditional values of *hiya, utang na loob*, Smooth Interpersonal Relations, and *bayanihan* are the basis of Filipino behaviour and harmonious relationships. These values combined with close family ties, deep and lasting friendships and a laid-back nature, make up the Filipinos today. Of course, with globalisation and exposure to other cultures, these traditional values are slowly being diluted. For example, some Filipinos, especially those in the cities, adhere to the western value of independence more than the traditional ways.

Hiya

Imagine having spent a whole day with your Filipino acquaintances only to discover they haven't told you about the bits of food stuck between your front teeth. Why didn't they tell you? Simple, it's the Filipino's value of *hiya* at work. While it is *nakakahiya* or embarrassing to have food stuck between your teeth, pointing it out would cause you even more shame or *hiya*. We are saving your feelings.

It is said that the Filipino's behaviour is governed by *hiya*. It defies translation but it is loosely taken to mean shame. *Hiya* is the uncomfortable feeling experienced when one performs a socially unacceptable action. Like their Asian counterparts, Filipinos fear 'losing face' and will always carefully consider what others will think. They will frequently exclaim *"Nakakahiya! Ano na lang ang sasabihin ng kapit-bahay"!* (How embarrassing, what will the neighbours say?). Filipinos are always carefully working on maintaining a good image to their relatives, friends, and neighbours. Breaking social taboos like taking drugs, failing in school, getting drunk, having a mistress, or getting pregnant before marriage are kept as secrets to preserve their dignity. If the secret is revealed, the person who performed the socially unacceptable act will experience intense shame. He or she will be embarrassed to face family, neighbours, and friends. To be called *walang hiya*, one who consciously performs a socially unacceptable act to offend others, is considered an insult.

Hiya drives the Filipino to act in socially sanctioned ways not easily understood by the foreign traveller. The following situations illustrate how our behaviour is governed by *hiya*:

- *Hiya* leads some Filipinos to borrow money or to go into

debt in order to avoid embarrassment. Such is the case during the town fiesta when each household is expected to prepare a feast. Even without sufficient funds, the head of the household would do anything just to have a spread on his table. It would be *nakakahiya* not to have a feast, even if it means borrowing money for the celebration.

• Giving an expensive gift to your boss even if you cannot afford it, because it will bring you shame to give a cheaper gift.

• Pretending to agree with your colleague. Openly disagreeing will put you or your colleague to shame.

• Pretending to understand instructions from your supervisor. Asking your boss to explain his instructions will indicate your failure to understand. This in turn envelops you in a cloud of shame. So instead of asking questions, you remain silent and instead, smile and nod in agreement. Later on, you try to figure out what the supervisor said. The same is true for Filipinos who don't understand what foreigners are saying. They just smile and nod even if they do not understand a single word.

It will take some time and a lot of getting used to before the Westerner comes to understand *hiya*.

4 dos & don'ts **in the PHILIPPINES**

DON'T, at all cost, cause the Filipino shame.

DON'T do anything to ruin your Filipino friend's reputation. Never put him or her in a bad light, as this will definitely bring about the unwanted feeling of *hiya*.

Let's say you saw your employee drunk and making a fool of himself the night before. Even if it is tempting to tease him about the incident, don't remind him of the embarrassing situation. Remember, Filipinos value maintaining a good image of themselves.

DON'T bring up embarrassing situations.

DO be careful in pointing out our flaws.

Most Filipinos will probably not tell you there is food stuck between your teeth. If it were the other way around, the Filipino would be extremely embarrassed if you pointed it out. Similarly, if a Filipino mispronounces a word, don't be quick to correct him. If he says "eh-pol" instead of saying "apple" gently, very gently, tell him "oh, you mean apple!" Better still, ignore the whole matter altogether. By correcting him in front of others, you draw their attention to his mistake. But there are no hard and fast rules here. Just be discreet and very sensitive when pointing out a flaw as this may cause much *hiya*.

Utang na loob

You've heard of the golden rule, "Do unto others what you want others to do unto you," right? Well in the Philippines, you can almost be sure your kind act will be reciprocated with another act of kindness. Filipinos have an interesting debt cycle called *utang na loob*. Again, there is no literal translation in the English language. It is a debt of gratitude for a good deed or an extraordinary favour done. Honouring

dos & don'ts **in the PHILIPPINES**

the debt of gratitude makes a lasting friendship.

Utang na loob has been ingrained in Filipino society for centuries. A classic example is when the newly elected mayor appoints to a top job a friend who helped him during the campaign. The mayor repays his *utang na loob* by doing his friend a favour. The cycle of debt payment does not end there. The appointed friend must continue doing favours for the mayor in gratitude. In response, the mayor keeps returning the favour. *Utang na loob* is a continuous cycle that never seems to end. It is never clear when a debt has been fully paid, so the relationship becomes an ongoing one.

This debt cycle may become tiresome at times. A wife once complained that her husband had been losing sleep repaying favours. Her husband's college education was financed by his uncle. Because of his *utang na loob* to his uncle, he cannot decline requests to write numerous business letters for him. Many years later, he is still repaying his debt.

A person who does not honour his debt or demands more than what was given, is considered *walang hiya*.

DO honour your *utang na loob* to others. When someone does a good deed for you, try to repay with kindness when you get a chance. You wouldn't want to be called *walang hiya*, right?

DO good deeds to others. You will definitely be rewarded by another kind act.

Smooth interpersonal relations

While Westerners often resolve conflict through direct confrontation, Filipinos do the exact opposite. They avoid face-to-face confrontations, instead they practice 'Smooth Interpersonal Relations' or SIR. This term coined by Frank Lynch, S.J., an anthropologist, refers to the Filipinos' unique ways of getting along with others in such a way as to avoid outward signs of conflict. SIR is based on an assumption that good relationships are without conflict and irritation. Confrontations, arguments and the like signify bad relations, so they must be avoided. If not, they will create an awkward situation and cause *hiya* for those involved. Filipinos have devised many ways to achieve social acceptance and maintain harmonious relationships. While they may seem more tedious than face-to-face confrontations for the Westerner, they come naturally for Filipinos. If you want to be accepted by Filipinos, learn the ways of SIR:

Pakikisama

Remember those times in high school when you and your gang of friends would agree to dress a certain way on appointed days? Even if you hated the outfit, you would still wear it for the sake of the group. In the Philippines, giving in to the group's wishes doesn't seem to end in high school. It is the essence of *pakikisama*.

Pakikisama means the ability to get along with others in order to avoid conflict. Individuals yield to the wishes of the leader of the majority, even though it contradicts one's wishes. *Pakikisama* operates among friends, especially a *barkada* (a gang or clique), families, even business associates. A student, who wishes to prepare for an exam, will watch a movie instead, out of *pakikisama*. An

individual who hates eating Filipino food will concede to his friends' wishes, because of *pakikisama*. Failure to cooperate with others is frowned upon.

Pakikisama propagates loyalty and cooperation among Filipinos. This powerful value may be beneficial or detrimental to the individual depending on the group's intentions.

DON'T insist on your own way all the time. If it will benefit more people, give in to the wishes of the group. Practising *pakikisama* will allow you to be easily accepted by Filipinos. For foreigners with a dominant independent personality, try to control your feelings and, if necessary, bite your tongue.

A foreigner's *pakikisama* is put to the test when his Filipino buddies are eating their favourite local food. While the food may smell terrible or appear disgusting to you, your friends love this stuff. In fact, they will offer it to you! They will understand if you decline, but you will win their hearts by tucking in just as they do. It will show you are *magaling makisama*, or can easily get along with others. And this is highly valued in our country.

8   dos & don'ts **in the PHILIPPINES**

Euphemism

Direct criticism will surely cause tremendous *hiya*. Instead, euphemism and indirect censure are employed. There are many ways Filipinos get the message across:

Teasing

A boss may jokingly say *"Ang aga mo, a!"* (Boy, you're early!) to her secretary, as she arrives terribly late. Teasing gets the message across without putting the person to shame.

The Ambiguous Yes

Filipinos utter "yes", even if they don't mean it. So it becomes a mystery if the "yes" could mean "yes" or "maybe", or "I don't know", or "if you say so" or "if it will please you" or "I hope you sense I mean no". Because of *hiya*, Filipinos have much difficulty saying "NO" outright. Uttering "yes" is an easier way out of a potentially awkward situation.

Even for something as simple as an invitation for dinner, the Filipino cannot say "no" right away. He will say "yes!" but have no intention of going. An invitation to dinner must be confirmed and pursued. Sometimes noncommittal replies like "I'll see if I can make it" or "I'll try to attend" are euphemisms for "I can't go, but haven't the guts to tell you so".

When the invitation is extended the second time, he will be ready with an appropriate excuse. So when a Filipino says "yes" to you, take it with a grain of salt. Ask questions to figure out what "yes" means.

White Lies

White lies are probably used throughout the world. But Filipinos may use white lies more than other people. Not that we enjoy lying, but it is easier than turning people down. Filipinos have much difficulty saying "you're not accepted" or "we're turning down your offer" or any other negative response. Doing so may be unpleasant for the recipient of the rejection. Instead of allowing this awkward situation from occurring, they would rather avoid the person. A number of excuses are made to avoid taking the phone call or worse, seeing the person face to face. After some time, the message gets across without directly putting the person to shame, but only after wasting a lot of time.

DO get the hint when your friend is constantly unavailable to take your call. Even if your friend has stomach problems, it would be an amazing string of coincidences that he is in the bathroom every time you call. It's not bad timing. He doesn't want to talk to you.

Timid Critics

While other cultures have no qualms criticising others openly, at times even to their face, the Filipinos have no heart to do this. When making a comment, Filipinos are scared to hurt others' feelings. They immediately utter a disclaimer in the beginning, "In my opinion…" This makes the person commenting less arrogant with his words, and it softens unfavourable remarks. A positive comment is first said before mentioning less favourable adjectives. Taking a bite of cake made by a friend, one would comment "Your cake was delicious, but the icing was too sweet". Other times an old saying *Bato, bato sa langit, ang matamaan huwag magalit* precedes the criticism delivered in front of a group of people. It translates to "Falling star in the sky, whoever it falls to should not be offended". This saying reminds whoever the criticism is intended for, not to be angered by the comment that follows.

Beating around the bush

Sometimes foreigners notice the Filipino exhibiting unusual behaviour. They may receive an extra-warm phone call or a visit without a specific purpose. The caller may keep talking for some time though you remain in the dark about the reason for the call. When you ask, "what can I do for you," the caller finally reveals a favour he is asking or donations he is soliciting. Some Filipinos masterfully mention their request at the end of their conversation, making it seem like an afterthought, for example, "by the way, Mr. Jones would you still be interested in buying raffle tickets for my church fundraiser?"

DO be patient when this happens. When a Filipino rambles on and on for no reason, take the cue and politely ask "how can I help you, Mr. So & so?" and he will soon spill the beans.

The Go-Between

When it is too embarrassing to ask a touchy question or discuss an awkward topic, Filipinos find a go-between. Since it is not appropriate for a young man to ask his first date directly whether she likes him, he cleverly finds a way to get feedback indirectly from her friend An employee who wishes to request a raise, courses it through her boss's confidante rather than actually asking her boss. Should the request be denied, it wouldn't be face-to-face. The go-between softens the blow.

Bayanihan

An extension of *pakikisama* is *bayanihan*. *Bayanihan* is working for the common good of the community. The trait is especially evident in the provinces where communities help each other till the soil or harvest crops. *Bayanihan* is best illustrated when neighbours help to physically carry a house (a *nipa* hut) to its new site. This spirit of cooperation is very much alive especially during calamities (which the Philippines has a lot of) and periods of crisis, where the whole community helps those in need. During the tragic earthquake of 1990, the *bayanihan* spirit saved the lives of many Filipinos trapped under collapsed buildings.

But it is the peaceful People Power Revolution in 1986 that best captures the *bayanihan* spirit. Filipinos non-violently protested against the Marcos dictatorship. Nuns, priests, teenagers and elderly, the rich and poor all stood together to regain Philippine freedom and democracy. For the benefit of the country, everyone did his or her share selflessly. Some bravely stopped military tanks, while others offered prayers, food, and cash donations. *Bayanihan* is probably the most positive value of the Filipino.

With the *bayanihan* spirit etched in the hearts of many Filipinos, charitable organisations remain popular throughout the country. These organisations do volunteer work to help the sick, the elderly, the handicapped, and street children. Fundraisers such as bingo socials or movie premieres are a roaring success.

DO be ready to lend a helping hand. Being sensitive to the people around you is key to acceptance by the local community.

It need not be as profound as caring for the sick and dying. It can be something as mundane as helping your neighbour start his car or supporting fundraisers.

Laid back nature

Relax… you're in the Philippines! Admittedly, it's not paradise. In fact, life can be difficult in these islands. But Filipinos have great ways of surviving difficulty and stress:

Humour

It's amazing how Filipinos can afford to smile or laugh in the middle of the most trying of times. During the darkest days of the Marcos administration, people circulated jokes, staged spoofs, and drew funny caricatures to cope with the situation. Even when everything seems to go wrong, the Filipino still manages to smile.

Bahala Na!

This phrase is a common expression uttered by Pinoys during the most trying times. *Bahala na* stems from *Bahala na ang Diyos* (God will take care of us).

Instead of facing the problem head on, they surrender it to God and let the situation take care of itself. Admittedly, it is passive and fatalistic. It does not give a definite solution to the problem, but it relieves Filipinos of making a decision and defending it to numerous friends and relatives. This *bahala na* attitude may be credited for helping many Filipinos come to terms with the seemingly hopeless times in their lives.

Time is relative

Filipinos used to be known to arrive late for everything. Well, times have changed. At least most business meetings and conferences start not too long after their scheduled time. But

dos & don'ts in the PHILIPPINES   13

generally, Filipinos are lax when it comes to arriving promptly. Coming ten to fifteen minutes later than the appointed time is acceptable. Besides you can be sure the Filipino has an excuse - blaming the traffic, the rain or some carefully crafted alibi.

DO allow extra time for traffic congestion when planning business meetings or arranging to rendezvous with a friend. Remember using the traffic for arriving late is an overused excuse already!

Parties and dinners don't start at the appointed time. If you arrive promptly you will be the first guest at the party. Even worse, your host may still be cooking dinner or getting dressed. They would panic at your unexpected early arrival and would be embarrassed for not being prepared.

DO arrive fifteen to thirty minutes after the appointed time for the party or dinner. This will be considered punctual.

Generally, the pace of doing business seems slower than more developed countries like the United States, Japan and Singapore. This can be quite frustrating for foreigners used to efficient service. When you have things repaired or made, don't expect it to be done on the appointed date. Let's say you need a pair of pants made by Saturday. Tell the tailor you need it by Thursday to be assured it will ready by Saturday. If you rely on them stitching your clothes by the date you need them, you will be very disappointed.

DO be very patient with the slower and, at times, indifferent service.

Chit-chat

Filipino have the gift of gab. They love to chat anywhere and any time. Even business meetings begin with chit-chat about the latest showbiz scandal, political controversy, or the latest fad. This puts those in the meeting at ease with each other and creates rapport among associates. Meetings also end with some small talk. Hence, real business is discussed between the chit-chat. Serious businessmen may think all the talking is a waste of time.

DO value these light-hearted conversations. Think of them as a vital investment for good business relations.

Close family ties

Family relations are treasured by Filipinos. In fact, one's identity is meshed with the reputation of the family. The Filipino family is not limited to father, mother and their children. Grandparents, uncles, aunts and cousins make up the extended family. Ageing grandparents stay with their son's or daughter's family. Westerners would be surprised to know that there are very few nursing homes in the Philippines. It is unacceptable to send one's parents to a nursing home, as it shows no *utang na loob* for the many years they cared for you.

Similarly, an unmarried sister or brother is also invited to live with the family of her or his married siblings. Uncles, aunts, and cousins are free to visit and join family events. The extended family is part of every single aspect of one's existence, be it happy or sad: birth, growth, sickness,

graduations, marriage, work, and death. Because of this close bond, the Filipino is rarely alone. Visitors are also treated like family to the dismay of some. They feel suffocated by the constant coming and going and interaction with their Filipino foster family.

DON'T get irritable if you feel smothered by hospitality and kindness. Retreat to your room for a few hours of being by yourself.

Elders are accorded with respect. Filipino children always seek their parents' advice on important matters. Parents never tolerate their children talking back to them or any adult for that matter. At an early age, children are taught to kiss their parents, grandparents, uncles and aunts on the cheek or have their hands touch the back of their elder's palm (*mano*) when they encounter them. This practice is continued throughout their adult life. Close friends of their parents are treated like *tito's* and *tita's* (uncle and aunts) and are accorded the same respect. Older sisters and brothers have the privilege of respect from their younger siblings. The older sister is lovingly referred to as *ate* and the older brother is affectionately called *kuya*. Just like other societies, younger siblings have to follow the orders of their older siblings. On the other hand, older siblings are expected to look after the younger ones.

DO treat your host family like your own family. As good hosts, they will treat you like a member of their own family. Grant them the same respect (or even more) you show your own family. Be especially respectful and courteous to the elderly. Be prepared to spend A LOT of time together.

Friendships

While family relationships are important, so are friendships. Each friendship is treasured and all efforts are made to make it endure through the years. You can count on the loyalty of your Filipino friend until the end. Through thick or thin, your Pinoy friend will be there for you. Friendships among Filipinos are so strong, even the families of friends develop a tight bond.

During teenage years, the Filipino has his close clique, a gang of friends or *barkada*. Some never outgrow the *barkada* and continue the friendships into adult years. Friends spend time drinking beer, playing mahjong or eating together regularly. But more than the fun times, friends assist each other with everyday problems. Favours are done for each other, even for the each other's families. Friends become almost like siblings.

DO give importance to your friendship with a Filipino.

You will surely make friends during your stay. Value your new found friends. Keep in touch with them and you will have a friend for life!

The *Manileño* & the *Probinsiyano*

The best advice to give visitors to the Philippines is to see the provinces. While most business activities are in Manila, the country's charm can be found in its beautiful countryside. Most provinces provide a welcome respite from Manila's traffic, pollution, and neurotic drivers. Even an hour or so away from Manila, visitors will be delighted to find fine beaches and quaint mountain towns. Even more captivating are the people in the provinces, exuding the warmest Filipino hospitality and genuine friendliness.

dos & don'ts **in the PHILIPPINES**

DON'T expect *probinsyanos* (country dwellers) to be just like the *Manileños* in appearance and behaviour, or vice-versa. The *probinsyano* has a simpler life and more conservative values than his urban counterparts.

DON'T make the mistake of expecting all *probinsyanos* to be alike. There are many differences within and among provinces.

Similarly, you, the visitor, are not expected to behave the same way in the city and in the provinces. Leave at home those groovy dancing shoes and revealing outfits when you go to the provinces. They may be inappropriate for some small towns. Dress in simple, conservative, comfortable outfits instead.

Body attributes

You're sure to notice that Filipinos make an effort to look good by dressing well and staying clean. But for them, the body is more than just appearance. Body parts are clear communication tools. If you find yourself nodding in agreement as you read this chapter, you are a keen observer. If not, watch the Pinoys and see their bodies at work.

Pointing with the mouth

Filipinos have a unique tradition of using the mouth to point out a direction. When asked for directions, he vaguely answers *doon* (there) then points his lips in the direction you should follow. With a few more questions, you'll be rewarded with more specific details.

DON'T mistake his pouting lips as getting ready to kiss you.

Eyebrow greeting

While Westerners say "Hi!", How are you?", "Hello!" and "G'day!" when they see a friend, Filipinos use their eyebrows. Upon seeing a friend or an acquaintance, as if on cue both eyebrows rise to acknowledge eye contact. A smile sometimes accompanies this greeting.

Staring is rude

As in most other cultures, staring is rude. But Filipinos cannot help gazing at foreigners, especially Caucasians. Filipinos admire their tall height and creamy white complexions.

DON'T feel offended when you catch them staring. An American executive was once caught inside a van in Manila's traffic jam. The next thing he knew a school bus full of kids was staring at him, delighted to see a Caucasian. Instead of getting irritated, he made faces back at them. This thrilled the kids immensely. Be flattered instead of annoyed, when people stare innocently.

dos & don'ts **in the PHILIPPINES**   19

DO smile or even better, make a funny face when you catch Filipinos staring at you.

Watch that finger

DON'T point at someone. It is considered ill mannered. Also, never use your middle finger for pointing or to call attention. It might be mistaken for an offensive gesture. If you want to call someone, beckon with the fingers moving in a downward motion.

Smiles

Some Asian cultures are wary of smiling, both giving and receiving, especially if they do not know the smiler. A natural reaction would be "what does he want from me"? Or, "Oh hell, he knows me but I don't remember him. Where can I hide!" But to Filipinos, smiling comes naturally. Even during a bad patch, Filipinos still manage to smile.

A smile is a pleasant greeting to friends, relatives and even strangers. Sometimes, the smile is a convenient mask for the Filipino when he is unsure or does not know what to do. Instead of asking a lot of questions which could embarrass him (remember *hiya*?) and the person he is talking to, he merely smiles. A smile is also a polite response when a Filipino does not want to commit, yet he does not want to embarrass the person asking. So whether you're happy, sad, nervous, confused or unsure, do as the Pinoys do - SMILE!

Physical contact among men and women

Filipinos are very tactile people. Parents frequently hug or smother their kids with kisses. Close female friends hold each other's hands when walking along the street or around the mall. Filipino males, on the other hand, are comfortable placing their arms over the shoulders of their friends.

DON'T get the impression that we're a nation of gays and lesbians! While many cultures would assume homosexual overtones, holding hands is socially acceptable in the Philippines as it is too in India, Bangladesh and other Asian societies.

When calling someone's attention, a light tap on the arm or elbow is used. A handshake is granted when meeting people. Other than that, avoid physical contact with the opposite sex. Unnecessary touching may be interpreted as a romantic liking for the person, or may even be considered offensive.

Passing in-between

Whether they are passing in between two people talking or someone watching TV, Filipinos will try to be as inconspicuous as possible. Because of their *hiya* to disturb people, they pass with their heads bowed, bodies slouched and their hands clasped together in front of them, saying "Excuse me, excuse me." They are doing their best to pretend they are invisible.

Scratching the head

No, it's not dandruff. When uncertain, confused, or they don't know the answer, Pinoys automatically scratch their heads, just like in the cartoons.

Cleanliness, good hygiene and looking smart

Filipinos don't seem to be affected by the grimy urban environment they often find themselves in. When it comes to their own homes and their own hygiene, you can be sure they are squeaky clean!

To counter the tropical heat and to feel refreshingly clean, Filipinos bathe frequently. Taking a bath at least once a day is a necessity, even when water is scarce. Some even bathe two or three times a day often using the native *tabo* or water scooper and pails of water.

Filipinos have no qualms about bathing anywhere at any time of the day or night. Males can bathe in public, wearing a pair of shorts of course. Women settle for small makeshift bathroom stalls, even with the threat of a Peeping Tom. They will do anything for a bath, as good hygiene is highly valued. Teeth are religiously brushed after every meal. Unwanted female body and facial hair are shaved or waxed regularly to appear neat

dos & don'ts **in the PHILIPPINES**

and clean. Body odour is taboo and considered embarrassing. Perfumes, colognes and deodorants sell well!

DO keep yourself looking neat and clean. Unkempt and grimy foreigners embarrass us.

Aside from smelling fresh and clean, Filipinos value looking good. Even with the tropical heat, they still manage to look smart. Men do away with jackets and ties for daily business meetings. Instead, a long-sleeved shirt and a tie, a fashionable shirt or the local long-sleeved polo shirt called the *Barong Tagalog* is the norm. Filipinas tend to follow the fashion of western societies. Employees of banks and government institutions and students are usually required to wear uniforms. It is essential for clothing to be clean and well ironed and for shoes to be spotless and shiny.

BARONG TAGALOG

During the Spanish era in the Philippines, Filipino males were ordered to wear their shirts untucked to clearly differentiate them from Spaniards. The creativity of Filipinos resulted in the birth of the *Barong Tagalog*, a long sleeved polo shirt made of pineapple, abaca, silk fibres, or cotton with hand-embroidered floral designs. A plain white collarless shirt is worn under the *barong* with dark coloured trousers. The *barong* is perfect for hot days in the tropics, as its natural fibres allow the body to breathe. It is still worn today by executives for business meetings and for special occasions like weddings and formal functions. Through the years, various styles have evolved. The casual short-sleeved version is called the *polo barong*. The formal *barong* made from pineapple fibres is called *piña*. The fine silk fibre also used for formal occasions is called *jusi*. So, leave those suits in the closet and start wearing the cool *Barong Tagalog*. Just remember, always wear it loose and untucked!

Beauty

Filipinos have a penchant for beauty and a high regard for beautiful women. Beauty contests abound throughout the archipelago. They range from the prestigious *Binibining Pilipinas* (Ms. Philippines) to smaller, humbler contests in the *barrio*. This fascination for beauty has expanded to Little Miss Philippines, Mr. Philippines, Pretty Boy, and even Ms. Gay Philippines!

Recognition for beautiful people does not end with beauty pageants. Attractive women are selected to participate in the town's religious processions or to become the muse of athletic teams and social organisations; or are encouraged to join show business (even if they can't sing, dance or act!). Parents are extremely proud when their child becomes a beauty titleholder, a muse, or a celebrity.

It comes as no surprise then to find a beauty parlour on almost every street corner. Those who can't afford the service of beauticians, rely on friends and relatives for grooming. They have no qualms being seen with curlers in their hair, seated comfortably outside their houses getting a manicure or pedicure while catching up on the latest gossip. You can even get a cheap manicure from enterprising beauticians aboard the lower class sea ferries - a rare phenomenon probably only seen in the Philippines!

RELIGION

Philippines

Religion is a crucial part of Filipinos' lives influencing as it does holidays, rituals, traditions, art, architecture, music, even dining habits. A basic understanding of our religion is essential for a better appreciation of Philippine culture.

The Philippines is by far, Asia's pre-eminent Catholic country. Its population consisting of over 80 percent Catholics is proof of the Spanish church's success in spreading the faith. Catholics have various religious groups including a very active charismatic group called *El Shaddai*, whose well attended services are often aired on television.

The rest of the population is made up of other religious groups of whom Muslims, constituting about eight percent, mostly reside in the southern island of Mindanao. About four percent of the population belongs to the Philippine Independent Church founded by Gregorio Aglipay as a nationalist Catholic Church in 1902. Another four percent are members of the *Iglesia ni Kristo* (Church of Christ), founded by Felix Manalo in 1914 based on a Unitarian interpretation of the Bible. Of course, many tribal communities still observe their pre-colonial belief in spirits, fairies, elves, deities, tree dwellers and other supernatural beings. Other Filipinos continue to believe in spirits and are intensely superstitious even though they were born into the Catholic faith. When asked why they still believe in superstitions, they rationalise *wala naman mawawala kung sundin* (there's nothing lost if we follow).

The majority of Filipinos have embraced the Christian faith, continuing the religious rituals and traditions introduced by the Spaniards. Catholic icons are visible everywhere: the crucifix, a painting or sculpture of the Last Supper or an image of the Virgin Mother and the Infant Jesus are displayed in almost every home. There'll be a rosary in the handbags of Filipinas. When startled, old Filipina women will unconsciously say *Susmaryosep!* - short for Jesus, Mary, and Joseph.

The truths of the Christian faith are contained in the Bible, and the guidelines for Christian living are summarised in the Ten Commandments. They are usually posted outside the churches as a reminder to all.

Non-Catholic visitors may be overloaded with all the unfamiliar icons, rituals, and traditions of the Catholic faith. There are some dos and don'ts to help you survive:

DON'T argue about religion with a Filipino. Filipinos are quite passionate about their faith and detest having face-to-face confrontations and arguments. So don't mix the two.

DON'T criticise the Pope. You might not agree with his views on family planning or sexuality, but keep them to yourself to avoid causing offence.

DO learn a thing or two about our faith. If a ritual is unclear, ask questions.

The following section should provide a good background on the basic elements of the Catholic faith.

Elements of the Faith

Many elements of the Catholic faith have become deeply etched in the lives of Filipinos:

Virgin Mary

The Virgin Mary is the patroness of the Filipinos with many icons all over the Philippines attributed to stories of her miracles. Each image is lovingly kept inside the church, an altar at home, or in a garden grotto. The devotion to Mary is so intense and widespread, you're sure to find someone praying the rosary in her honour anywhere, at any time of the day.

Santo Niño

The oldest Saint in the Philippines is a toddler! As early as April 28, 1565, an image of Jesus Christ as an infant was discovered. It is assumed to have been left by an early European expedition. The young Christ is called the *Santo Niño,* meaning *child saint.* The image of the first Santo Niño can still be seen in Basilica de Santo Niño in Cebu City. The original icon of the Santo Niño is garbed in a rich Flemish costume with velvet cloak and a red plumed hat. His left hand holds the globe with a small red cross and the right hand is slightly raised in greeting. Today, the image can be found in churches, houses, shops, even in jeepneys, sometimes dressed as a doctor, fireman, or whatever is the profession of its owner!

It comes as no surprise that the Feast of the Santo Niño celebrated on the third Sunday of January is very popular. The festivals in honour of the young Christ in Tondo, San Beda, Aklan, Cebu and Pandacan are much awaited and widely attended.

Novenas & devotees

Filipinos lift up all their problems to the Lord in prayer. Oftentimes, a nine day prayer or novena is offered for the attainment of a fervent wish. Filipinos have novenas for everything: for the impossible to Saint Jude; for illnesses and for passing the licensing board exams to Our Lady of Manaog; for lost items to Saint Anthony... Probably the most popular devotion is to the Black Nazarene, which is enshrined in the main altar of Quiapo Church in Manila.

The Black Nazarene or *Nazareno* in Pilipino, is an image of Christ dressed in a purple robe carrying the cross. The Spaniards brought this statue from Mexico in the seventeenth century. Every day, but especially on Friday, thousands of Catholics pay homage to this miraculous image. Devotees line up behind the main altar to kiss, touch or wipe the feet of the dark Christ with their hankies. This is followed by praying the rosary or novena or sitting quietly in adoration. In the middle aisle, devotees slowly advance on their knees towards the altar, focused in prayer. Some women even don purple dresses like the Nazareno in fulfilment of a vow. On January 9th, the day of the district's fiesta and on Holy Monday, devotees from all over the country troop to the church for a massive procession. If you think traffic is bad in Quiapo on Fridays, you ain't seen nothing yet!

Just like Quiapo, traffic is bad in the Baclaran area of Manila every Wednesday when devotees pay homage to the Mary, Mother of Perpetual Help.

Priests & nuns

Priests and nuns are accorded much respect in the Philippines. Many religious orders are responsible for the Christian education in private schools of middle class and elite children. The priests are well known and well loved in their communities. Even with a Chinese surname ironic for a religious leader, Cardinal Sin, the former Archbishop of Manila, is well respected and can influence the President's decisions on important national issues.

DO treat priests and nuns with respect. Just like the rest of the community, respect the religious. Greet them "Good Morning!" or "Good Evening!" as the case may be. Most would be delighted to show you around their church and will treat you graciously as well.

dos & don'ts **in the PHILIPPINES** 29

Churches

The more than three hundred years of Spanish rule has left the Philippines with hundreds of churches. But in the past century, many have been destroyed and replaced with modern structures. Oftentimes, the church is the centre of town and always filled with life. Droves of families flock there on Sundays, some even on weekdays. The church is central to Filipinos as it is the setting for the most important events in their lives: baptism, first Holy Communion, weddings, even wakes and funerals. Churches are treated with respect.

DO visit the historic churches in the country. Ilocos, Rizal, Laguna, and Bohol are noted for their remarkable centuries old churches. Throughout the country, you will be pleasantly surprised to discover beautiful places of worship.

DO observe silence inside and around the church. Respect the worshippers who are intently praying. Refrain from talking or laughing. Turn off your Walkman or Discman. Beeper and cellular phones should be silenced as well.

DO wear decent clothing. When entering churches, it is essential to wear modest clothes. This means do not wear tattered clothes or those which reveal too much flesh. Sleeveless shirts, shorts, and mini skirts are not acceptable in some churches. Jeans and shirts are, but just be sure they are clean. During holidays, beautiful dresses for women and smart looking shirts for men are expected.

DO check whether the service is said in English, Tagalog, or the local dialect if you wish to worship. Consult the hotel or resort front desk personnel. If they are not sure, ask them to call the church for you. Though the readings and songs sound just as lovely in an unfamiliar dialect, it would be sad to attend mass when you don't understand a word.

DON'T take anything from the church. If you want a souvenir, take a photo or purchase something from the parish store. Thefts are common in churches, especially from those in the provinces. Many religious objects are priceless and irreplaceable antiques. Remember the sixth commandment, 'Thou shall not steal.'

DO ask permission to go up the bell tower. Most churches in the Philippines have them affording the best view of the whole town. Some allow visitors to go up to get a good view and to see the old bells. Be aware though, that you must be physically fit to climb many steep steps. Other churches keep the bell towers off limits to the public, since they are very dirty and full of bats.

Asking Permission for Photography

With the impressive details inside and outside the churches, you'll surely be enticed to take some souvenir photos. Most churches are left open throughout the day so devotees can freely come in to pray. Usually, you may take pictures.

DON'T take photos if a mass is in progress. It can be very distracting and annoying for the priest and those praying.

Passing a church? In respect for holy places, Filipinos make the sign of the cross whether they are driving or walking past a church.
Your first time to visit a church? Say three Hail Mary's, three Glory Be's, and three Our Father's, and make three wishes. With the great number of churches in the Philippines you can visit, you will probably run out of wishes.

Mosques

Particularly in the southern island of Mindanao, Islam has a popular following. When going to a mosque, the following guidelines should be noted:

DON'T enter if there is a religious gathering in progress, unless you are Muslim. Even then, you must know what the gathering is about. Be aware that mosques are usually full on Fridays, when congregation prayer happens in the afternoon.

DO take a bath before going to the mosque. Islam requires a clean body in prayer. Even if you are not Muslim, please observe this simple necessity.

DO put on a hat if you are male. You'll notice that Muslim men wear a flat cap when they pray. A baseball cap is not acceptable.

DO be almost fully covered if you are female. A scarf over your hair should not be overlooked.

DO remove all footwear before entering the mosque proper.

DO secure approval for photography; otherwise stick to the outside scenery.

HISTORY OF THE FILIPINO PEOPLE

Philippines

It's always good to know the history of the country you are visiting. While there will be no exam when you arrive, it will give you a better appreciation of the people, the monuments, the museums and the events and festivals you're bound to encounter during your stay.

Brief Philippine History

Pre-Spanish Times

There are no written records of Philippine history prior to the Spanish era. However based on archaeological finds in the Philippines, it appears that ancient man lived here as early as 50,000 years ago. The aboriginal inhabitants called *Negritos* or *Aetas* arrived 30,000 to 25,000 years ago. The Indonesians and Malays arrived between 3,000 B.C. and 500 A.D. Trade relations with the Chinese were recorded in 900 A.D., but may have existed as early as the 4th century. Arab traders and missionaries arrived in 1200 A.D., spreading Islam to the Southern Philippines by the end of the 13th century.

Spanish Times

In the early 1500's, Spanish explorers arrived,

claiming the islands for Spain. By the late 1500's, large portions of the country were under Spanish rule. Catholicism, the galleon trade, and a feudal system were all introduced.

The late 1800's saw the birth of national consciousness and an awakening of Filipinos to the abuses of the Spanish government and church. Jose Rizal, the Filipino national hero, was responsible for the awakening of the people through his reformist novels, *Noli Me Tangere* and *El Filibusterismo*. He was executed by the Spaniards in 1896, which led to the Philippine revolt against Spain. June 12, 1898 marks Philippine independence from the Spaniards who lost to Filipino and American forces.

American colonisation

The Americans gained control of the islands after Spain formally sold the Philippines to them. While the Filipinos continued to fight for their independence by resisting their American colonisers, they lost the Philippine American war in 1901. The American government worked to make improvements in economic development and social progress in the country. Their most notable contributions were the introduction of the public school system and democracy. A commonwealth government was in place by 1935 with President Roxas as the first elected Filipino president. During the Second World War, Japanese forces attacked the Philippines. This marked the beginning of Japanese occupation in 1942. Two years later, American forces liberated the Filipinos from the Japanese.

The Philippine Republic

In 1946, the Americans finally granted the Filipinos independence and the Philippines was established as a Republic. From 1946 the country has been led by elected Filipino officials. In 1972, President Ferdinand Marcos declared Martial Law. A period of restrained press freedom and rampant abuse of authority followed. Political detainees without due process of law, numbered in thousands, including opposition leader Senator Benigno 'Ninoy' Aquino. His assassination in 1983 led to protests and an awakening to the unjust acts of the Marcos government. Three years later, snap elections and a peaceful revolution drove Marcos into exile.

President Corazon Aquino succeeded him. Her six year term as President was quite eventful with the approval of a new constitution in 1987, a 7.7 intensity earthquake in 1990, the closure of the American military bases, the eruption of Mount Pinatubo in 1991, and several failed coup attempts. Fidel Ramos succeeded the first woman president in 1992. Six years later, action star-turned politician, Joseph "Erap" Estrada won the presidential elections. He in turn was removed early 2001 after a damaging impeachment trial into allegations of massive corruption. His former Vice President, Gloria Arroyo, succeeded him.

DO read as much as you can about the Philippines before heading there.

DO call the nearest Philippine embassy or consulate for specific travel inquiries.

DO talk with friends or acquaintances who have visited the country. Their stories will give you a sneak preview of what's in store for your trip. But remember your experience will be different from theirs. It can be better or worse…depending on what you make of your trip.

ACCOMMODATION

Philippines

Whether you're staying short term or long term, in a hotel, resort or even an apartment, keep in mind:

Safe keeping

DON'T leave valuables in your room. Remember the hotel staff has easy access to your room. While most are trustworthy, not all are. It is best to leave your passport, jewellery, traveller's cheques, and other important documents in the hotel safe box. But, hand over your possessions only to reputable hotels. If you have doubts, take your valuables wherever you go in a handy belt bag.

DO write the contents of the safety deposit box on a piece of paper and have the receiver sign. Keep this piece of paper so you may hold the recipient responsible for any lost item.

DO keep your luggage locked when you leave the hotel room. Leaving your things scattered around the room makes it more tempting for the maid to liberate your possessions.

Bill details

DO check details of your bill. You may have been incorrectly charged for services you did not avail of. Also, check the accuracy of the telephone charges. You wouldn't want to pay for phone calls you didn't make.

38   dos & don'ts **in the PHILIPPINES**

Phone cards

DO purchase a phone card at any souvenir shop, news stand or bookstore. It will save you a lot of money to use a pay phone, rather than paying the hotel's exorbitant phone rates. A pay phone can usually be found in the hotel lobby.

No local female guests

DON'T bring female guests to your room. You wouldn't want to come to harm by being drugged or robbed, would you? Also, most hotels would like to maintain a good reputation, so some have plain clothes security stationed on every floor to prevent entry of prostitutes. Should a female guest stay too long in your room, the hotel security would not hesitate to knock to check if everything is fine.

Bare facilities

DO check the facilities of the hotel before making a reservation or checking in. In some remote places, basics like hot water, a shower and a phone are not included. It would be nice to know in advance if you have to bathe using a pail and *tabo* (water scooper) or if you have to make do with an electric fan instead of an air conditioner!

dos & don'ts **in the PHILIPPINES**   39

Staying with a local

DO accept an invitation to spend a night or two at a local's house if you can trust your new found friend. With the Filipino's famous hospitality, it comes naturally to locals to offer a bed to visitors. Many backpackers claim they never had to sleep out in the open in the Philippines, unless it was their choice. There was always a farmer or fisherman offering to share his humble hut for the evening. Keep in mind that women should always exercise caution in accepting an invitation.

Motel?

DON'T expect to find weary travellers taking a break from long drives in a motel!

In the Philippines, a motel is not a low-price hotel for travellers. Instead, it is a rendezvous for lovers! Rooms are rented by the hour and are specifically designed for short intimate escapes. Since most guests are secret lovers, the motels are constructed to keep their meetings discreet. High walls permit entrance and exit with minimum visibility. A private stairway from their garage leads the star-crossed couple to their love nest. Since it is taboo to be seen driving out of motels, couples try to disguise themselves by wearing sunglasses or pretending to read the newspaper. Sneaky couples taking cabs, slouch and only reappear when they are well away from the motel.

DO stay away from motels unless you have a romantic evening in mind.

Location, location, location

DO check the location of the hotel. Remember the traffic situation in Manila is horrendous.

Most businessmen prefer staying in Makati, Manila's central business district. The Ortigas area in Pasig is fast becoming popular among visiting businessmen as well. Choose a hotel close to your activities. You wouldn't want to spend most of your time sweating it out in traffic and spending most of your money on cab fares, would you?

Location is also very important when looking for a beach resort. When making phone reservations, always check the hotel's location. You think you're getting a bargain, only to find your resort situated far from the beachfront. Instead of hearing the calming sound of waves, you'll be awakened by noisy tricycles. You wouldn't want this to happen!

Personal Security & Safety

Keep these three basics in mind:

DO lock all doors and windows at all times, especially before you go to bed.

DO know where the fire exits are.

DON'T reveal the name of your hotel and your room number to strangers.

dos & don'ts **in the PHILIPPINES**   41

Staying for a long time?

DO check for the following when looking for a place to rent: water supply problems, telephone, leaks, flooding, hot and cold water, shower, air conditioning and security.

Be warned that some places in Manila do not have water throughout the day. While a phone service is a basic necessity, it is scarce in some places and can take years to be installed. Heavy rains hit Manila from June to September, so check the roof for leaks. Roadworks fronting the house may seem temporary, but months and years may pass before they are completed. Most importantly, the house or apartment you are renting must be safe!

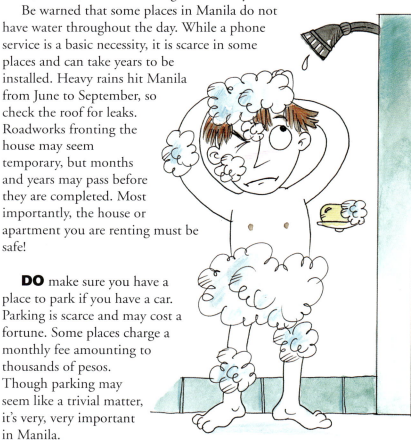

DO make sure you have a place to park if you have a car. Parking is scarce and may cost a fortune. Some places charge a monthly fee amounting to thousands of pesos. Though parking may seem like a trivial matter, it's very, very important in Manila.

DO check out garage sales. Usually, expatriates conduct garage sales to dispose of their belongings before heading back to their home country. You'll find good quality appliances and furniture (sometimes even a car) at cheap prices.

CELEBRATIONS

Philippines

The Filipino people's joyous nature blended with close knit families and communities, results in a number of celebrations and gatherings. Any event becomes an occasion for a celebration. As visitors develop close relations with Filipinos, it is most likely you'll be invited to a baptism, a wedding, a birthday party, a house blessing, a blowout, a *balato*, or a *despedida*. Do join in the festivities!

Baptism

The actual sacrament of baptism takes place in a church, usually the parish of the child, followed by lunch or dinner at a restaurant or the house of the child's parents. Friends and relatives of the newborn's parents are invited to join in the celebration.

DO accept the request to be a godparent. It is an honour to be selected as one. Turning down the request would cause *hiya* to the parents of the child. Aside from giving birthday and Christmas gifts to your godchild, a special relationship must be built with the child and his/her parents.

DO attend the baptism ceremony and the feast.

DO dress in semi-formal clothes.

DO give the child a gift. Traditionally,

44 dos & don'ts **in the PHILIPPINES**

godparents give a silver cup, or spoon and fork set, or a pair of gold earrings. In recent years, practical gifts like a stroller, a high chair and crib are more appreciated. Generally, anything nice for the child is appropriate.

DO bring some small change if you are godparents. Parents and godparents shower small change as a wish for prosperity for the child.

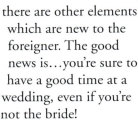

DON'T join in picking up the coins on the floor. Usually, only children and teens scramble for them. It would be embarrassing to be the only adult fighting for a few pesos.

Weddings

Filipino weddings are similar to western weddings with some subtle and not so subtle variations. The wedding gown, the wedding cake, the souvenirs, the reception are all there. But wait, there are other elements which are new to the foreigner. The good news is…you're sure to have a good time at a wedding, even if you're not the bride!

DO attend the church service and join the festivities at the reception. The reception is

dos & don'ts in the PHILIPPINES 45

usually held at a hotel, a fancy restaurant or a social club.

DON'T feel bad when you are not invited to join the group photos in the church, right after the mass. Usually, only the families of the bride and groom are included in the formal souvenir shots in front of the altar.

DON'T expect any wild drinking. It is usually a very happy wholesome gathering of friends and relatives.

DO wear a suit or a *Barong Tagalog* for men, and a stylish formal dress for women. Avoid wearing black since the festive occasion calls for brighter colours. Members of the entourage are usually dressed in the wedding colours seen in the invitation. Guests are welcome to wear the wedding colour as well, but are not required to.

Gifts

DO present the couple with a gift. These days, couples register at department stores and select which presents they like. You may purchase one of these preferred gifts to suit your budget.

DON'T give knives or pointed objects, as they are believed to lead to a broken marriage.

DO leave the gifts at the table near the entrance of the reception hall as you

arrive. You may opt to send the gift to the house of the bride or groom, depending on who invited you.

DO give a more substantial gift if you are a sponsor. As in baptisms, celebrities and high ranking officials are often selected as sponsors or *ninongs* & *ninangs*. Based on the photos on the society pages, the former President Estrada must have been a *ninong* dozens and dozens of times already. This must be the price of being popular.

DON'T come late. Only the bride is allowed to be late for her wedding. The bride must not arrive too early as she will appear too eager. A very important sponsor (say, the President of the Philippines) may get away with arriving later than the bride.

DON'T sit at the head table unless you are asked to. Honoured guests are seated together with the bride and groom at the head table, often called the presidential table.

DO congratulate the groom.

DON'T congratulate the bride. Instead offer her good wishes. It is seen as the young groom's victory in conquering the heart of his young bride. If you are a male friend or relative of the bride, you may plant a gentle kiss on her cheeks. Remember she is now married. A kiss on the lips is reserved for her husband only!

dos & don'ts **in the PHILIPPINES**

Some Filipino Wedding Traditions & Practices

1. Pamanhikan
Before all the wedding preparations, the groom must first obtain his bride's hand in marriage. The groom and his parents go to the bride's house to formally ask the bride's parents permission to wed their daughter.

2. When to wed
June weddings are not popular in the Philippines because of the rainy season. December is the most popular and practical choice for couples because it is cooler and not usually rainy and most family members are in town for the Christmas festivities.

It is bad luck for siblings to marry in the same year. The older one gets to marry first.

3. Unlike western societies, it is the groom's family that shoulders most, if not all, the wedding expenses.

4. For the bride -
- It is bad luck for the bride to try on her gown prior to her actual wedding day or the wedding will not go through.
- Wearing pearls on her wedding day will bring her many heartaches and tears in her married life.

5. Rice, flower petals, or confetti are thrown over the couple as they leave the church. This is meant to bestow prosperity and fertility on the couple.

6. A meal is served for guests to partake in, either lunch or dinner. It may be buffet or a sit-down meal.

7. After the meal, some rituals are done:
- Guests ding their glasses with their spoons to signal the bride and groom to kiss.
- The newly married couple cut their wedding cake and romantically feed each other a mouthful or two.
- After the customary messages from the best man and the father of the bride to the couple, they lead the guests in a toast.
- Sometimes, a giant bell is constructed with two doves inside. The bride and groom pull the ribbon to release the doves. Another variation is to have the couple hold the doves and make them kiss, then release them.
- Young unmarried females approach the head table to pull out ribbons sticking out from the wedding cake. Each ribbon is attached to a foil embedded in the cake with a wish inside, something like Chinese fortune cookies.
- Just like American weddings, all single women gather together. The bride stands with her back towards them and throws her bouquet. The lucky lady who catches the bouquet will be next to marry. A parallel custom is for the groom to remove the garter worn by the bride and throw it back over his shoulder to the unmarried male guests. Again, the one who catches it is next to marry.
- A romantic song is played, and the young couple head to the dance floor for the first dance. Guests join the couple on the dance floor once the first song is over.

Money dance

In the provinces, the newly married couple dances during the wedding reception. While they are dancing, guests pin peso bills to their clothes as a present. Some even give U.S. dollars to the delight of the young couple (as they are worth more!). At the end of the dance, the bride's dress and the groom's *Barong* are filled with money bills.

DO join in this unique Filipino wedding tradition. Go ahead and pin a couple of money bills on the newly married couple's clothes.

Pictures

Filipinos are photo-crazy, especially during weddings. Professional photographers are usually hired to document the event in pictures and in video.

Souvenirs

Young sisters, nieces, or friends of the bride go around distributing small souvenirs of the occasion. It can be anything the couple fancies: a rosary, a box of chocolates, or small glass trinkets. It usually has the couple's names and the date of the wedding printed on it. Usually, only women are given souvenirs.

Wedding anniversaries

Filipinos do not stop at celebrating their wedding. Years later, wedding anniversaries are commemorated with big parties especially the silver (25th), the ruby (40th), and the golden (50th) wedding anniversary. Some couples even renew their vows and re-enact their wedding with their children and grandchildren in attendance.

DO give the couple a present in accordance with the anniversary motif, silver for the 25th anniversary, something red for the ruby, and so on.

Birthdays

Filipinos, like all other people, celebrate their birthdays. Unlike the tradition in many countries, the birthday celebrant is expected to treat family and friends to lunch or dinner. Some prepare a simple snack for their officemates. But, every single birthday party must have a noodle dish.

DON'T cut the noodles, as Filipinos believe to do so will shorten the life of the celebrant.

DO give the birthday boy or girl a gift when invited to the party or dinner.

DON'T expect the celebrant to open your gift in front of you. It's not that she does not appreciate your gift, it's just usually done privately. Filipinos are not comfortable when gifts are opened, as they feel the other guests assess them. Opening a modest gift may embarrass the giver and a substantial gift may shame guests who gave smaller ones.

DON'T open your gifts in front of all your party guests when you have your birthday party.

House blessings

When Filipinos move to a new house, they have a house blessing. We believe it is not proper to live in a house unless it is blessed in the presence of friends and relatives who will wish them prosperity. Prayers are said and a priest sprinkles holy water in every corner of the house. Important guests hold candles, which are provided by the host. After the blessing, there is dinner.

DO bring a hearty appetite for the feasting after the blessing. You may also bring a house warming gift, but this is not expected.

Aside from houses, people also have their offices, stores, and even cars blessed.

DON'T be surprised to see a priest circling a brand new car and sprinkling it with holy water.

Blowout

A happy event such as a job promotion, a birthday, or getting honours in school is a good reason to celebrate. All these times are occasions for a blowout, a treat sharing the honour and happy moment with friends and relatives.

DO blowout friends when you experience good fortune. They will be thrilled to share in this happy occasion.

Balato

Filipinos enjoy betting - from the lottery, sweepstakes, horse races, cock fighting to even guessing the last digit of the winning score in a basketball game. Oftentimes, they lose. But winning calls for a celebration or *balato*. Friends and family expect a piece of the winnings.

Despedida

A person moving abroad or to a far-off place is given a *despedida* or farewell party by family and friends. You need not give a gift, just be there to say goodbye.

A *despedida de soltera* is a party given by the parents of the soon-to-be bride in her honour, as she bids her single life goodbye.

CINEMA

Philippines

The cinema is probably the most popular form of entertainment in the country. Filipinos love movies, from Chinese martial arts flicks to Hollywood blockbusters to local comedies and dramas. English flicks from Hollywood make their way to the Philippines just a few months after release in the United States.

National Anthem

DO stand in respect for the national anthem played prior to the screening of the last full show. Some theatres play it at the beginning of every movie. Theatre, concerts and dance performances also play the anthem before every show.

Eating in Movie Houses

DON'T be surprised when you see people having a picnic inside the movie house. Aside from popcorn, potato chips, and candy, some Filipinos eat their lunch or dinner while watching the movie. Filipinos eat just about anything, anywhere, at anytime of the day - while watching a movie is no exception!

All day movie

DO be warned that people may walk in at any point of the movie. Unlike western movie houses where most people arrive at the start of the film, local movie houses allow entry at any point as long as seats are available. You can stay on for the next movie and the next and the next... So, one movie pass allows you to watch the same movie over and over again throughout the day. This is something visitors find phenomenal.

Smooching

For young couples, the last row in the movie house is the perfect place for some lip action. It is dark, with cool air conditioning, and no moviegoers behind them to complain. When the last row is taken, they just have to settle for any other seats in the movie house.

Movie Stars

Movie stars have an incredible following in this country. After making a name in the movies, they graduate to politics. Their popularity allows them to garner more votes than well-respected lawmakers. Filipinos have no qualms electing an action star for President, a comedian for Senator and a drama actress for Mayor.

Sex & Violence

Philippine cinema has it all: sexy films, action films, dramas, comedies, even spoofs of Hollywood blockbusters. Producers will do almost anything to bring more people to the movie theatres. Riding on Titanic's phenomenal success, a whole movie spoofed it, aptly called Tataynik.

DINING PINOY STYLE

Philippines

Filipinos love to eat. But for the visitor, dining Pinoy-style takes some getting used to. You may be revolted to eat *balut*, the infamous fertilised duck embryo much beloved by Filipinos, or worse, partaking of man's best friend, dog meat. Do not fear: pets and other exotica are very unlikely to appear on the menus where you eat. Dining in the Philippines is a very pleasurable experience. Visitors are bound to enjoy the refreshing drinks, the large variety of tropical fruits, the freshest seafood, the delectable meat dishes and the sweet confections. Dining Pinoy-style is not just about taste. It also involves colour, texture, aroma and even the wrapper of the food. It's truly a complete sensory experience.

The Pinoy meal

Filipinos eat breakfast, lunch, dinner, and a snack called *merienda*. Just like the inhabitants of this archipelago today, Filipino cuisine is a mix of indigenous and foreign influences, particularly Spanish and Chinese. Here is some useful information when eating a Pinoy meal:

HOW to EAT :

Praying before meals

Most Filipinos silently give thanks to God for their food before they eat. So don't be shocked if your companion suddenly makes the sign of the cross and silently utters a prayer before eating.

DO be silent and politely wait for the prayer to end before you dig in.

58   dos & don'ts **in the PHILIPPINES**

Eating with spoons and forks

Most Filipinos, especially those living in Manila, use a spoon and fork for eating. Knives are rarely used. The fork, in the left hand, is used to slide food, especially rice grains, to the spoon. So don't be surprised to find yourselves struggling to cut your meat with a fork and spoon. But don't worry, knives are available when requested.

Kamayan (eating with hands)

DO try eating with your hands or *kamayan* style, as Filipinos traditionally do. It requires some practice to press the food together and shoot it to your mouth without making a mess. In the provinces, most people still eat this way. In Manila, *kamayan* is rare but there are still some restaurants in the city where you eat with your hands.

Using condiments or *sawsawan*

For the Pinoy, no meal is complete without the sauces or *sawsawan* (as it is called in Pilipino). *Patis* (fish sauce), *toyo* (soy sauce), *suka* (vinegar), *bagoong* (shrimp paste), *sili* (chilli), and *kalamansi* (local lemon) are used to complement the taste of the main course. Filipinos mix these sauces to make the perfect *sawsawan* suited to match the main dish. Unlike other chefs, the Filipino cook does not mind the diner altering the taste of his food. In fact, a small saucer is usually placed beside the plate for the diner to prepare his/her special *sawsawan*.

dos & don'ts in the PHILIPPINES   59

DON'T miss a Filipino meal where you can concoct your own *sawsawan*. You're bound to enjoy the experience. Soon you'll find yourself constantly preparing a *sawsawan* for every meal.

Banana Leaves

They're not just essential attachments to banana trees. Banana leaves have a number of uses in Filipino kitchens: to line pots to prevent food from burning; to add flavour to steamed rice; to wrap native delicacies; as an environmentally friendly packaging for meals; and even as a plate when you eat *kamayan*. Can any other leaf do all that?

No slurping, please

While in some Asian countries, you'll find diners slurping their food to show their enjoyment, this is not the case in the Philippines. Filipinos find it offensive to make slurping sounds when eating.

DON'T make noises with your mouth when you eat.

DON'T order noodles if you're a slurper!

Finish your food

Filipinos value food. They love an abundance of it and hate to see food go to waste. Leftovers are reheated and eaten for another meal, or are cleverly transformed into another dish.

DO finish the food on your plate.

DO give it away if you are stuffed.

DON'T ever throw it away, unless it's spoiled.

WHAT to Eat:

Rice

Filipinos are hearty rice eaters from breakfast to dinner. The typical breakfast consists of garlic rice, a viand of marinated fried fish, beef or pork, and a fried egg. Lunch and dinner also consists of rice and an *ulam* or viand.

For a Filipino, no meal is complete without rice. Even if they enjoy eating a burger, they don't find it as satisfying as a meal with rice. To stop that between-meal energy crunch, Pinoys also snack on a variety of rice cakes (*bibingka, suman,* and *puto*).

Seafood

Surrounded by water, Filipinos are blessed with the bounty of the sea. All sorts of fish, crabs, lobsters, squid, mussels and even oysters, make their home around our shores. For most Filipino families living near the sea, fish and rice are eaten daily. Having constant access to the freshest seafood, Filipinos usually prefer to cook it simply: grilled, fried, or boiled in soup. There's no need to mask the flavour in complicated recipes.

Meat

Pork, chicken and beef are readily available in almost all areas. In the provinces, goat, deer, *carabao* (water buffalo) and some exotic meat are eaten too. Almost always, meat is eaten with plain

dos & don'ts in the PHILIPPINES   61

white rice. Since meat is expensive, it is usually served only during special occasions, like fiestas. Furthermore, almost nothing is wasted when the animal is slaughtered. The creativity and frugal ways of the Pinoy cook has concocted tasty dishes using the tongue, blood, intestine, liver, lungs, tail and other offal. Several meat dishes are altered Spanish recipes.

DON'T serve pork or cook with pig products if your Muslim friends are coming to dinner.

Vegetables

In a predominantly agricultural country, it comes as no surprise to have an abundance of vegetables. In the provinces, most families grow them in their own backyards. Vegetables are rarely eaten raw in a salad. Almost always, Filipinos prefer them cooked and served hot. For most families, a vegetable dish saute'ed or cooked with coconut milk, is the main course eaten with the staple, rice.

Desserts

The sweetest reminders of the centuries of Spanish rule are the irresistible desserts adapted to local ingredients. After a hearty Filipino meal, sweets are necessary to cleanse the lingering flavours left in the palate. It can be anything sweet from a healthy tropical fruit to a sinful creamy confection.

DO forget your diet and sample the different sweets and desserts available in the provinces. Each province usually has its own sweet speciality. You must try the all time favourite desserts like Leche Flan, Sorbetes, Pastillas, and Polvoron.

DON'T forget to try the tropical fruits of the islands:

Bananas, mangoes, jackfruit (*langka*), soursop (*guyabano*), coconut (*buko*), durian, rambutan, *sinuegulas, duhat, chico.*

Just a few words about DURIAN

Durian is a fruit found in the southern island of Mindanao between August to October. This very large, heavy green fruit with spikes would kill you if it dropped on your head! To find durians in the city, just follow your nose to the source of an intense sweet sickly odour. For many people, Asians included, the smell is nauseating. Inside is a fluffy yellow mass of creamy flesh wrapped around large brown seeds. Not many Filipinos like the taste. Just like gourmet food, the taste of this aphrodisiac is acquired. Durian fanatics would say "it stinks like hell, but tastes like heaven". If you become addicted to this fruit, be aware that most airlines and hotels ban this "skunk of the orchard" because the smell lingers for days. One last tip, to rid yourself of the potent scent, wash your hands in and gargle water poured in the empty durian husk. The distinct odour and flavour magically disappears.

dos & don'ts **in the PHILIPPINES**

Popular Filipino dishes

Chicken & Pork *Adobo*	This is a very popular dish flavoured by soy sauce, vinegar and garlic, stewed over a slow fire.
Kare-kare	Oxtail and vegetables stewed in a rich sauce of ground peanuts and toasted ground rice.
Tinola	Clear chicken stew with potatoes or green papaya.
Sinigang	Bouillabaisse using fish, prawn, or meat with vegetables made sour by adding some acidic fruit like tamarind.
Pancit	Noodles adapted from the Chinese with a Pinoy taste. There are many variations of the noodles, garnishing and flavourings.

Common ways of cooking

Prito	fried
Ginisa, gisa or gisado	saute'ed
Paksiw	stew in sour fruit or vinegar
Adobo	saute'ed in garlic or vinegar. Anything can be cooked adobo-style: vegetables, meat or even peanuts
Inihaw	grilled over charcoal

IN-BETWEEN MEALS

Merienda

Filipinos are voracious eaters, often eating a snack between meals called *merienda*. Farmers used to eat breakfast as early as 4am, making their stomach growl by 9am. This started the morning *merienda*. In between the long hours between lunch and dinner, there is the afternoon snacking session. *Merienda* fare may be a sandwich, rice cakes (*kakanin*), *pancit*, a cup of soup, street food... anything that satisfies the hungry Pinoy.

Street Food

To satisfy the insatiable Pinoy, there is a wide variety of snack foods peddled in the streets. Some of the street food is guaranteed to intrigue you:

Balut - boiled ducks eggs with embryo eaten with rock salt

Taho - a soft creamy tofu with tapioca and caramel syrup

Fishballs - small air-filled fried fishballs

Dirty Ice Cream / *Sorbetes*

Home made ice cream available in local flavours: *keso* (cheese), *tsokolate* (chocolate), *gatas* (milk), avocado, *ube* (purple yam), *langka* (jackfruit). It's called "dirty" since they are not made by big commercial ice cream companies.

dos & don'ts **in the PHILIPPINES**   65

Banana-Q - fried sweetened cooking bananas on a stick

Turon - Banana or yam fried egg rolls

Barbecue - Marinated pork cubes are skewered on a stick, grilled over charcoal, and sold in makeshift food stalls along the road. There are other parts of chicken and pork, which are grilled and sold with such clever names:

Adidas	Chicken feet
Betamax	Chicken blood clots
IUD	Chicken intestines
PAL*	Chicken wings
Helmet	Chicken head
Walkman	Pig's Ears

named after Philippine Airlines

DO be careful. The government does not monitor street peddlers. They do not have sanitary permits.

Turo-turo stalls or *carinderias*

Along the streets, small eateries serve a number of cooked Filipino dishes. These establishments are called *carinderias* or *turo-turo*. You check out the line up of ready to eat food and point to your choice, hence the name *turo-turo* (point-point).

Again, these small stalls have no sanitary permits. To be assured of freshly cooked food, order dishes which are grilled or fried on the spot.

Exotic Filipino food

Filipinos eat some food which may seem strange or look unappetising to the visitor. Don't fret. Not all locals eat these mysterious dishes. In fact, not many of us have tried them. But before you say "No!" to a plate of strange looking delicacies, learn a few little things about some exotic food of the archipelago. Who knows, after reading this you may be daring enough to sample one or two dishes!

Azucena or dog meat

Yes, some macho Filipino males eat man's best friend. It is a popular *pulutan* or canapé to go with rounds of gin. Dog meat is most popular in the Mountain Province, where dogs are raised for eating.

Betute

In the province of Pampanga, small frogs are stuffed with ground pork and deep-fried to a crisp.

Kamaru

Also in Pampanga, mole crickets that burrow in the moist soil of the rice fields are the perfect match to beer. Heads and wings are discarded. Their bodies are boiled in vinegar and garlic until tender, then saute'ed in lard, onions, and tomatoes.

Manggang Hilaw at Bagoong

Crisp unripe green mangoes dipped in *bagoong* is a favourite of women. Pregnant women, it is said, often crave for the sour flavour of the mango blended with the salty taste of shrimp paste. Visitors find themselves squinting at the tart taste of this Filipino favourite.

Lechon

The whole pig roasted on a bamboo pole for special occasions like fiestas, weddings, and parties. First, everyone takes a piece of the crisp and succulent skin eaten with a sweetish liver sauce. Then, all partake of the special juicy meat under the skin. **DO** try it. It's quite delicious and very tasty!

Filipinos are thrilled when foreigners sample their cooking especially the exotic food. But they would understand if you politely decline. Remember, *pakikisama*? You will immediately gain acceptance and endear yourselves to your local hosts if you eat what they eat.

What to drink?

DO drink bottled mineral water from the grocery. Tap water may not agree with your stomach.

DO replenish lost fluids with fresh juices and shakes from fresh tropical fruits like *buko,* pineapple or mango. Try cool refreshments like *mais con hielo, sago't gulaman,* and *halo-halo.*

Alcoholic drinks

Filipinos are heavy drinkers. The local beers and gin are quite strong. In the provinces there is a wealth of potent fermented drinks. Don't underestimate these local brews, they have a high alcohol content.

DO think twice before you challenge a Filipino to a drinking match.

One last tip before you dig in

When you chance upon a Filipino eating a meal or a snack, you will immediately be invited to eat. Often times, they do not have enough food to share, so politely decline. If they insist that you eat, accepting a drink would be fine. Filipinos usually serve their guests the best. They would be embarrassed to serve you their everyday fare.

EMERGENCY

Philippines

We hope you won't need this section.
But still, read the tips.

DO keep the numbers listed below handy. Jot them down on a piece of paper to pop into your wallet for easy reference when you need it.

For fires, poison, accidents, robbery, ...

117	STREET WATCH - 24 hour hotline
166	Emergency Police Assistance - 24 hour hotline
524-1078 **521-8450** loc. 2311	National Poison Control Information Service
244-4141 **244-4545** **244-5151**	Association of Phil Volunteer Fire Brigades, Inc.
160-16	Association of Volunteer Fire Chiefs & Fire Fighters of the Philippines, Inc.
524-1660 **524-1728** **523-8411** **523-8412**	Connects you to the 24-hour Tourism Assistance for lost or stolen passports, travellers cheques, and personal belongings. Complaints against local residents and commercial establishments can be filed here. These reports are handled by tourist police investigators and operatives.

70 dos & don'ts **in the PHILIPPINES**

In times of illnesses or accidents

There are more than a dozen hospitals in Metro Manila. These hospitals have well trained medical practitioners and satisfactory medical equipment. Check yellow pages for hospital listing.

During an emergency, it's best to proceed to the Emergency Room of the hospital. With Manila's traffic situation, it usually takes a long time to wait for the ambulance to come and collect you.

If you are staying at a five star hotel, most have a clinic with a nurse and a doctor. You would be relieved to know that the medical expertise in Metro Manila and Cebu City are comparable to the top hospitals in other countries. Unfortunately, this cannot be said of most provinces. Rural areas don't have adequate medical facilities. Some *barrios* don't even have a single medical doctor.

If you get sick, get treatment from a Filipino doctor before heading home. They will be more familiar with tropical illnesses than their foreign counterparts.

Lost credit cards

Lost credit cards or traveller's cheques must be immediately reported to their respective issuers:

AMEX	814-4666
Citibank VISA & MasterCard	813-9333 in Manila
	255-9333 in Cebu

For lost airline tickets or changes in schedule

Call your airline. See the local yellow pages directory.

For those who wish to stay longer

Contact the *Commission of Immigration and Deportation (CID)* immediately to extend your visa: 5273265; 527-5376; 527-5371; 527-5372; 527-5378

For any problem, contact your embassy or consulate

They are ready to assist their nationals especially in times of trouble. See the Yellow Pages for complete listing of Embassies.

> ***For additional phone numbers,** check the yellow pages or dial 1-1-4 for directory assistance in Manila.

Remember: **DON'T** panic! There will always be someone to help you in times of a crisis. You just have to ask.

FIESTAS & FESTIVALS

Philippines

An old Spanish saying says "When the fiesta comes, everything has a sparkle to it. It is the right time to meet Filipinos at their best".

Fiesta, or *pista* in Tagalog, means celebration. It is more than a party. It is when the whole community joins together for up to three days to celebrate the feast day of the town's patron saint. A fiesta showcases the best the town has to offer: warm hospitality, talented and friendly people, the best fruits and vegetables of the season, the famous sweets, biscuits, crafts, and the most delicious cuisine.

So, experience the best Filipinos have to offer. Take up friends' offers to attend the fiestas in their respective hometowns. Or check the list of fiestas a few pages from here and disappear to the provinces to witness this joyous spectacle.

Since the fiesta aims to feature only the best, it requires months of preparation. For nine consecutive days prior to the patron saint's feast day, devotees troop to the church offering *novena* prayers and women start preparing ingredients for all the dishes to be cooked for the banquet. Houses are cleaned, as it is *nakakahiya* for guests to see unkempt homes. Streets are decorated with bamboo arches and buntings. On the eve of the fiesta, there is usually a dance or a beauty contest. The culmination of a fiesta is the religious procession of the patron saint clad in his or her finest clothes.

DO make it a point to experience a fiesta where the best of the Filipino radiates! Everyone is welcome. May is the most popular month for celebration, but there is usually a fiesta going on somewhere in the archipelago throughout the year. Be aware that festivities are more subdued during lent. There is no merry-making and no dancing, in respect of the solemnity of the Lenten season.

DO expect the traffic to be worse than usual. If it takes three hours to get to your destination on an ordinary day, it may take six hours on the day of the fiesta. City dwellers who join the celebration clog the usually quiet provincial streets. Some roads are also closed for the procession. It's a good idea to get to the fiesta a day or two before it begins. This way, you'll get a chance to witness the pre-fiesta preparations and activities too.

DO wear comfortable shoes. Expect to do a lot of walking. Since it's unlikely you'll be able to park your car close to the action, you'll find yourself walking to the centre of town. Throughout the day, you'll be wandering from one house to another, to the church and to other parts of town.

DO join in the festivities, but do not be too rowdy. Remember that this is a religious celebration. Respect the religious symbols as they are carried during the procession. If the community is reciting a prayer, be silent and listen.

DO be prepared to eat, eat and eat. Filipinos serve their finest food during fiestas. None is

dos & don'ts **in the PHILIPPINES**   75

complete without *lechon* (roasted pig). It is as important to the Filipinos to have *lechon* on fiestas as it is for Americans to have turkey on Thanksgiving or ham at Christmas for Europeans. There seems to be an endless supply of food. The hosts make sure they never run out, as it is embarrassing to do so (remember *hiya*). If there is insufficient food, it will appear as if the host did not prepare for the fiesta, or worse, has no money for this special occasion.

DO accept an invitation from a stranger to join the banquet. If a local person finds out you have not eaten lunch or have no place to go for lunch, you will surely be invited inside their house for a meal, even if you are a stranger. This is Filipino hospitality at its best. For the foreigner, even for the Manileño, this seems like a dubious act. You may initially think the villager has malicious intentions towards you. Don't worry. Their only desire is to make you feel welcome in their town. But, never walk into a local's house without an invitation. It is simply rude and improper.

76   dos & don'ts **in the PHILIPPINES**

DO expect a lot of people! Students and adults working far away return to their hometown for this special event. Many foreigners and Manileños come to join in the fun as well.

DO bring lots of film. Fiestas are full of colour and life. There will be many photo opportunities.

DO bring drinking water and a change of clothes. With the heat and all the action, you will surely be perspiring at the end of the day.

DO understand the significance of the fiesta rituals: sometimes it is not appropriate to join in. In the town of Obando, women who have difficulty conceiving offer a dance to the patron saint of the town. In doing so, they believe they may easily conceive a child. Unaware of this, a male visitor who joins in the dancing will look foolish.

dos & don'ts **in the PHILIPPINES**   77

Some Filipino Fiestas & Festivals

January 9   **Black Nazarene Procession**
Thousands of Catholics crowd around the streets of Quiapo in Manila when the Black Nazarene, the over one hundred-year-old life-size statue of Christ made of Blackwood, is carried throughout town. A motorist's nightmare!

Third Sunday of January
Sinulog
An annual festival in Cebu where people dressed in costume gather downtown marching or dancing the peculiar Sinulog steps to honour the Santo Niño, the child Jesus. Hotels are nearly always booked out on this weekend. Smaller-scale Sinulog festivals are celebrated in Kabankalan, Negros and Dipolog, Zamboanga del Norte.

Third Weekend in January
Ati-atihan
A Philippine-style mardi-gras in Kalibo, Aklan with three days of dancing, singing and drum beating. Thousands of people outrageously costumed and cleverly masked and blackened with charcoal celebrate round the clock until the last evening when a long procession ends the festivities.

January or February
Chinese New Year
Depending upon the lunar calendar, Chinese New Year celebrations take place between 21 January and 19 February. Traditional dragon dances and Chinese rituals are performed in Manila's Chinatown to usher in good fortune for the new year.

February (movable)
Bamboo Organ Festival in Las Piñas
Ten days of musical performances showcasing the unique bamboo organ found only in Las Piñas.

February (movable)
Panagbenga
A week long flower festival in the mountain city of Baguio.

February 22-25
People Power Revolution Anniversary
This remembers the peaceful end to the Marcos era. Every year a mass followed by a street party are held in EDSA, the historic site of the People Power revolution. Participants usually don the popular yellow shirts worn during the rallies against Marcos dictatorship.

March/April (around Easter)
Moriones
In the island of Marinduque, a colourful week long play re-enacts Christ's passion.

Throughout the month of May
Flores de Mayo
Throughout the country, little girls and young ladies clad in beautiful gowns offer flowers to the Virgin Mary late in the afternoon or early evening.

Throughout the month of May
Santacruzan
A re-enactment of Reyna Elena's (Queen Helen) search for the cross upon which Jesus Christ was crucified. The most beautiful lady is selected to portray Reyna Elena. Other lovely ladies join in the procession as well.

May 14   ### Carabao Festival
The *Carabao* - the water buffalo - the farmer's best friend, is groomed, decorated and paraded around the town of Pulilan, Bulacan. The highlight is seeing the *carabao* kneel before the church and compete in races.

May 15   ### Pahiyas Festival
In thanksgiving to San Isidro for the bountiful harvest, the

patron saint of farmers, the towns of Lucban and Sariaya in Quezon happily celebrate his feast day with processions. The façade of houses are creatively decorated with agricultural products and *kiping*, a wafer-thin bunting made from rice paste dyed in warm colours and hung in various shapes and sizes.

May 17-19 Sayaw sa Obando
During these three days, a series of dance processions are offered in Obando, Bulacan. On May 17, young unmarried men dance in the street while praying to find a bride. The next day is the turn of single young women. Finally, on the last day childless couples perform a fertility dance in their desire to have children.

June 24 Feast of San Juan Bautista
A wet and wild feast day in remembrance of St. John the Baptist held in San Juan, Metro Manila. Water is thrown at passing cars and everyone else. Be prepared to get wet.

In Balayan, Batangas, it's a 'dry' but mouthwatering celebration. Instead of throwing water, the parade of *lechon* (roasted pigs) highlight this day.

October 10-12 Zamboanga's Hermosa
Cultural performances, religious ceremonies, exhibitions, regattas, and beauty contests are held in Zamboanga for its patron saint, Nuestra Señora del Pilar.

October 19 Maskara
On the weekend closest to October 19th, the biggest festival in the Negros Province happens in Bacolod city. Street dancers wear costumes and smiling masks.

December 24 Giant Lantern Festival
The most spectacular lantern parade and contest in the Philippines takes place in San Fernando, Pampanga. The giant *parols* (coloured paper lanterns) measuring over ten feet in diameter come to life in a spectacular synchronised show of lights and sounds.

FRIEND'S HOUSE

Philippines

It is most likely that you will be invited to a friend's house for a home cooked meal or to spend a few nights with his or her family. As a house guest, the whole family will make an effort to ensure your stay with them is as pleasurable and comfortable as possible. Often times, a member or members of the family will give up their bed for you to sleep on. You will be served only the finest food, given the best chair in the house, and be asked to stay in the most beautiful portion of the house. The family will be embarrassed to show untidy parts of their home.

DON'T expect all Filipinos to live in *nipa* huts. Although there are still folks who reside in these airy dwellings especially in the provinces, most city dwellers live in concrete structures. If you wish to experience life in a *nipa* hut, visit one of the many beach resorts using this cool architectural style.

The Anatomy of the Pinoy House

The Filipino house is uniquely built to suit the particular daily needs of the Pinoy.

High walls - These walls surround the house and lot to prevent burglaries. Unfortunately, burglars have become quite good at climbing walls.

Gates - The Filipino house usually has two gates. A gate enabling vehicles entry and exit to the lot, plus another gate for entry and exit of people.

Living room - Guests are received in the living room usually resplendent with framed photos of family members. If the family can afford it, they have a piano in this room (even if no one plays the instrument).

Dining room - This is where guests partake of special meals. Some families only use the dining room when there are guests, otherwise they dine in the kitchen.

Kitchen - The Pinoy house usually has two kitchens: the clean and the dirty kitchen. Guests are allowed inside the clean kitchen.

This is where the wife can occasionally show off her cooking prowess and fine kitchen appliances. But in reality, the action is more often performed by the maid in the dirty kitchen. It is embarrassing or *nakakahiya* for the owner of the house when guests see the filthy kitchen.

Laundry area - This is where the maid washes and irons the family's laundry. Pinoys have a laundry woman or maid to wash their clothes.

Garage - Leaving the car in the streets is often unsafe. You may find your stereo or other parts of your car missing, or worse, your whole car may disappear.

Phone - Surprisingly, not all homes in Metro Manila have phones. With the entry of new telecommunication companies in recent years, some households who waited for years to get a phone line finally have phones. But many others are still waiting.

Water - For an archipelago surrounded by water, it is strange to have a water shortage. There are some households where water is available only at certain hours.

Bathroom - Unlike Western homes, it is rare to find a bath tub in a Filipino's house. While many middle class homes have showers, this is not the norm. Some families use a pail and a *tabo* (water scooper) when they take a bath. If there is not enough water, the shower becomes useless, and you have to resort to this traditional method.

dos & don'ts **in the PHILIPPINES**   83

DO bring a token or small gift for the family or your host. A box of chocolates is acceptable as are flowers.

DO arrive with a hearty appetite. Filipino hosts constantly feed their guests until they are stuffed. Also, it is embarrassing for the host to run out of food, so an abundant spread is prepared. It is customary to offer guests some extra food for their homeward journey. If they notice you liked a particular dish, some will surely find its way into your luggage to take home.

DON'T rush to the buffet table when dinner is served, even if you are starving. You will appear too eager and deprived of food. Only after some prodding by your hosts is it acceptable to head to the dinner table.

DO sample all the food. Most dinner parties are buffet-style, where there is an abundance of food to choose from. Your host will carefully observe which dishes you sample. And as a lot of effort is exerted preparing each dish, they'll want you to sample all.

Even if you are just dropping by for a few minutes, it is common courtesy for Filipinos to serve you some refreshments, usually a glass of juice or Coke and a sandwich. Whether it is a simple or elaborate snack, you must take a bite to show you appreciate the gesture.

DO greet the elderly members of the household. They may not

join the conversation, preferring to sit on the sidelines, but make it a point to greet them and to say "goodbye" when you leave.

DON'T drink too much. Your friend's family would not be comfortable to have a drunken guest.

DON'T expect the dinner party to start on time. Guests show up late because punctuality may give the impression of over eagerness for social acceptance or to get to the food first.

DO sit where you are asked to sit. Do not stroll around the house. There are some areas which the host would not like the guest to see.

Staying for the night, can I bring a friend?

A problem might arise when you want to bring an uninvited friend along. If he or she is the same sex, it might place a burden on your friend as you are the only one wanted. If the uninvited friend is of the opposite sex, some real problems will arise.

The difference lies in the fact that in western society, a host will allow the guest to sleep on the couch or anywhere the guest indicates. In Filipino society, a guest is treated like royalty and the best the family can give will go to the visitor. Unless the host family is very wealthy, there are usually no guestrooms in Filipino homes. So mom and dad might give up their room for the their son and his guest, while they sleep elsewhere. Now, how can the son sleep with a male guest who has a female companion? In Philippine society, it is impossible for the three of you to sleep in the same room in a respectable house. If your host gives up his room for you and your sweetheart, he will have to sleep somewhere uncomfortable. You wouldn't want that, would you? Also, you most certainly will not be welcome to sleep there again.

Before bringing a friend where an overnight stay is intended, it is best to consult with your host. If your host does not know your friend and you have never seen your host's home, drop the idea of bringing him or her. This would be better than taking an uninvited stranger along and creating an awkward situation.

Beds

In some Filipino homes in the provinces, there are no beds. Instead, a *banig*, a mat made of woven dried leaves is laid out on the floor and presto, you have a place to sleep. If you're used to sleeping on soft mattresses, you'll probably have a sleepless night.

But if you have back problems, this is perfect for your posture.

Wear acceptable clothing

No matter how hot it is in the Philippines, it is still uncommon to sleep merely in one's underwear or in one's birthday suit.

DO wear decent clothes for sleeping as well as lounging around the house. The heat may be tempting for women to wear skimpy shorts and tight tank tops and for men to walk around the house barechested. Don't give in to temptation or even be a temptation for your Catholic hosts. Remember, most Filipinos are still generally conservative!

The Maid (also referred to as "helper" or *katulong*)

Many Filipino families employ the services of a maid who stays with them. They become part of the family, assisting the mother in household chores: preparing meals, cleaning the house, doing the laundry, and looking after the kids. When you need something, do ask your host. He or she may ask the maid to do it, but the best recourse is to ask mother rather than giving orders directly to the maid.

dos & don'ts **in the PHILIPPINES** 87

Slippers

Almost all Filipinos use slippers inside their house to keep their homes free of street grime.

DO remove your shoes before entering their home.

DO bring your own slippers should you be staying overnight.

FUNERAL & THE WAKE

Philippines

If you are staying for a year or so, you will probably experience the wake or funeral of a colleague's departed relative. What happens on such an occasion? What should you wear? How should you act? The answers to these questions are found in this chapter, so read on . . .

Filipinos share every event in life, even death. Family and close friends immediately gather together to commiserate with the kin of the deceased. Family members take turns to stand vigil over the corpse day and night for up to three days before burial. Card games and mahjong keep awake those holding vigil throughout the evening.

Even when mourning the death of a parent, sibling or relative, the same warm Filipino hospitality is extended by offering food or drink to any visitor who drops by. The wake in the Philippines may not appear solemn to the foreigner, but Filipinos try to maintain a less boisterous air and exhibit a sense of loss true to the spirit of the occasion.

DO send flowers or a Mass card offering prayers for the departed. An *abuloy* or cash donation to defray burial expenses is offered to families in financial difficulty.

DO go to the wake to offer condolences and spend a few minutes comforting your bereaved friend.

DO avoid wearing brightly coloured and casual clothing. Family members are expected to wear black, especially during the funeral.

DO attend the funeral, starting with a Mass in the funeral parlour or church and continuing to the cemetery where the body is buried.

Some Pinoy folks beliefs on death

1. The family of the deceased is prohibited from bathing, cleaning the house or cutting hair during the wake (especially if it is held at home). To do any of these may cause death to another family member.

2. Omens of death
   - pet dog continually digging
   - presence of a black moth or butterfly
   - dream of losing a tooth (may be negated by telling someone about the dream)
   - scent of candles

3. Catholics put a cut rosary on the hand of the corpse if she is a woman, and a cross for men. The rosary must be cut to end the death, because the rosary is an endless cycle.

4. Candles and flowers must be left at the cemetery and should not be brought into the house as this may lead to another death.

5. Mourners must not return home straight from the wake as it will bring death into the house. Stopping by a coffee shop or restaurant is usually practiced.

While none of these beliefs is preventive, they persist. As old folks say "nothing is lost by observing them."

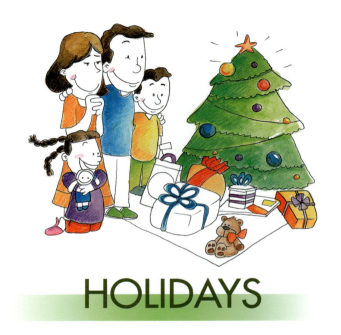

HOLIDAYS

Philippines

Just like other countries, the Philippines has its own set of holidays. It is advisable to know when banks, offices, and services shut down and what happens on these special days.

Public holidays

On public holidays, all offices and banks are closed. Most restaurants, shopping malls and department stores remain open except during Maundy Thursday, Good Friday, Christmas and New Year's Day.

January 1	- New Year's Day
February 25	- People Power Anniversary
Maundy Thursday*	- Thursday before Easter
Good Friday*	- Friday before Easter
Easter Sunday*	
April 9	- Bataan Day
May 1	- Labor Day
June 12	- Independence Day
November 1	- All Saint's Day
November 30	- National Heroes' Day
December 25	- Christmas Day
December 30	- Rizal Day

Moves each year: based on Catholic Church's liturgical calendar

Other public holidays may be announced upon the discretion of the President. There is also some hype for commercial occasions like Valentine's Day on February 14th and Halloween on October 31st, especially in bookstores, department stores, restaurants and shopping malls. A number of Filipinos enjoy celebrating these events too.

New Year's Day

For the first-timer, witnessing New Year's Eve in Manila is bound to be an experience in sensory overload. Filled with excitement, Filipinos welcome the New Year with a lot of noise, lights, food and family traditions. Everything is done to rid the bad spirits of the previous year and to bring good fortune for the New Year.

DO be an active spectator in ushering in the New Year. Eat, drink, and be merry. Part of the fun is doing all sorts of silly and not so silly things to ensure more food and more money in the year ahead.

Here are some fun New Year's eve beliefs & practices you can do:
- Jumping up and down at the strike of midnight will make you grow taller.
- Eating twelve round fruits such as grapes will bring you good luck.
- Pockets filled with coins will ensure a financially prosperous year.
- Lights all switched on, all drawers pulled out, all doors flung open, objects with covers uncovered, and windows opened. All these are believed to bring luck, but it usually just brings in smoke and dust from fireworks.
- Wearing polka dots will make you rich, as the circles resemble coins.

dos & don'ts **in the PHILIPPINES**

DON'T light that firecracker.

It has been a tradition to ward off bad spirits with noise. Unfortunately, firecrackers have caused many accidents among kids and adults in the past years. If you want to make lots of noise, use a car horn or bells instead.

Lent

Since the majority of Filipinos are Catholics, lent is observed throughout the archipelago. Lent is a forty day period beginning on Ash Wednesday, culminating on Easter Sunday.

DO know that Catholics are encouraged to abstain from eating meat during all Fridays of Lent.

DO be aware that the festive mood of the islands shifts to a serious tone as Filipinos participate in the solemn Lenten rituals:

Ash Wednesday

On this day, Catholics attend mass and are blessed with an ashen cross drawn on their foreheads to remind them they are from dust and from dust they will return. This is a day of fasting.

Palm Sunday

Palm leaves are waved by the crowd during the mass as a dramatic remembrance of Jesus Christ's entrance into Jerusalem and the true beginning of His final week on earth. The creativity of Filipinos transforms the traditionally plain palm leaves into intricately woven designs. The leaves are sold outside churches to be blessed during the Palm Sunday mass. Once blessed, they are placed on the doors or windows of houses to ward off evil spirits.

Holy Week

Maundy Thursday to Easter Sunday constitutes Holy Week. The entire week is marked by a number of events remembering Christ's suffering such as the *pasyon*, sung readings of Christ's passion, and the *Senakulo*, passion plays presented nightly. The washing of the feet and the Last Supper are remembered on Holy Thursday. On Good Friday, the crucifixion and scourging of Christ are re-enacted by devout Catholics throughout the country, complete with self mortification and the shedding of blood. Some Filipinos are literally nailed to a cross. Others are crowned with thorns, and still others inflict pain on themselves.

Some Catholics prefer less painful Lenten traditions such as *Visita Iglesia*, where they visit seven different churches on Holy Thursday. If completed, their wish offered in prayer will be granted. Aside from attending religious services and performing observances, adults are also required to fast and abstain from meat on this day. Others choose to abstain from other pleasures of life such as smoking or drinking throughout the duration of lent.

The *Salubong* caps the Easter celebration when, at dawn, a little girl dressed as an angel stands on an elevated contraption to reveal the image of the Resurrected Christ and an image of his jubilant mother right outside the church. The solemn ambience is quickly replaced by a festive mood.

DO expect Manila to be deserted from Maundy Thursday to Easter Sunday. Families take advantage of the long weekend to leave the city.

DO witness the serious side of Filipinos. The mood is solemn during this week. Churches are packed. Television stations and radio stations either stop normal programming to give way to religious shows, or go off the air altogether.

All Saint's Day

Families pay respect to their dearly departed by lighting a candle and bringing flowers to their tombstones. Some even stand vigil with food, a radio and a pack of cards for entertainment. The mood is more festive than solemn. It's almost like a picnic with vendors roaming the cemetery grounds and burger and pizza huts erected specially for this annual event. Parking inside the cemetery is almost impossible.

Christmas

It is said that Filipinos celebrate the longest Christmas season in the world. As early as September, preparations for the Yuletide Season begin, ending on the feast of the Three Kings on the first Sunday of January.

Misa de Gallo

Starting December 16, for nine consecutive mornings, dawn masses are offered. They are called *Misa de Gallo* or gift masses. Devotees pray for a wish to be granted, something that can only happen after completing all nine. Traditionally, masses were scheduled at 4 am, so farmers could return to the fields soon after. These days between 4 am and 5 am is more common. *Puto bumbong* and *bibingka* (rice cakes) sold outside the church are the perfect breakfast rewards for rising early for *Misa de Gallo*.

Midnight Mass

A mass is offered on Christmas Eve. Families attend this special mass dressed in their finest clothes.

Gift-giving

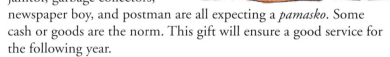

DO give gifts to friends and relatives, plus all those you have *utang na loob* to, be it your boss, officemate, neighbour or even the laundry woman. The maids, security guard, janitor, garbage collectors, newspaper boy, and postman are all expecting a *pamasko*. Some cash or goods are the norm. This gift will ensure a good service for the following year.

DO start shopping as early as October to avoid the mad rush at the malls during December. There are Christmas bazaars held as early as September where you can find export quality items or imported items at discounted prices.

Parols

Houses and buildings are adorned during the Christmas season with fancy versions of the star or what Filipinos call the *parol*. In remembrance of the bright star that led the three kings to the Child Jesus on the first Christmas Eve, local artists came up with the *parol*. Made of coloured pieces of paper, sometimes illuminated by light bulbs inside, the *parol* is displayed during December or even earlier to add colour to this festive season. Malls, streets, and

dos & don'ts **in the PHILIPPINES**

buildings are adorned with tiny Christmas lights and *parols* in various sizes, shapes, and colours creating a visual spectacle. The province of Pampanga, about an hour's drive from Manila, is best known for creating these lovely Yuletide decorations.

DO hang a *parol* outside your house and office during the Christmas season.

DO check out the Giant Lantern Festival where huge *parols* are paraded in the town of San Fernando, Pampanga.

Belen

Local craftsmen create replicas of the nativity scene consisting of the holy family, three kings and all the farm animals present during the first Christmas Eve. This nativity scene, the *belen*, may be crafted from wood, ceramic, paper mâché, whatever the local artist fancies. Trust Filipino ingenuity to come up with creative renditions of the *belen*. A small version is found inside homes while larger versions decorate churches and buildings.

Family reunions

The holidays are a big time for family reunions. The whole clan spends Christmas Eve and Christmas Day together feasting on the finest food, talking, laughing, and opening gifts. The traditional Christmas spread consists of ham, cheese, apples, grapes, and chestnuts, just like in Western homes.

DO bring a gift for your host when invited for Christmas lunch or dinner. Unless you are close to all the family members, you are not expected to bring gifts for each one. A cake, chocolates, or a basket of fruit for the family will do.

LANGUAGE

Philippines

In a country with over seventy dialects, one would expect difficulty communicating with the locals. Not in the Philippines, even with Pilipino (or Tagalog) as the national language, English is widely spoken throughout the islands. However, there are still subtleties of communicating with Filipinos, which may confuse visitors.

Filipino English

The majority of Filipinos can understand and speak English. In fact, English is used when conducting business. Correspondence and contracts are almost always written in English as are most road signs. Because of this, many expatriates live in the country for many years without learning to speak or read Pilipino fluently.

Many Manila residents have mastered a perfect American diction and accent. Yet there are some that speak English with a different tune. They apply the intonation and pronunciation of the language they speak in their locality, when conversing in English. So the visitor will probably hear spoken English sounding like a song and the letter "f" replaced by "p".

Be aware that Filipinos tend to be more familiar with American rather than Australian or British accents and vocabulary.

DO speak slowly and use simple words if you want to be understood.

Peculiar Pinoy lingo

Filipinos have accorded some English words with new meanings:

C.R.	Restrooms are called C.R. short for comfort rooms.
Joe	All Caucasian males, sometimes even females. (This is an effect of the GI Joe of World War II. Once the Caucasian is introduced to them, Joe is replaced by his real name.)

Soft drinks   Instead of soda or pop.

Take-out or Take home   Instead of saying 'to go', to signify you'll eat your meal elsewhere.

Filipinos sometimes call cameras "Kodak", toothpaste "Colgate", soft drinks "Coke", and tissue paper "Kleenex". So powerful is the brand association for these products, they have become generic names.

Common Filipino Expressions you're bound to hear. After hearing these frequently, you might find yourself using them, too:

Hoy!	Similar to "hey you!" when you are calling someone in a crowd.
Psst!	A hissing sound to call attention of companions.
	All the hissing and whistling can be quite annoying and alarming at times, but it succeeds in grabbing your attention.
Kwan	Loosely translates to *"whatchamacallit"*. It replaces the word you can't remember. When referring to a table from a place whose name you can't remember you would say *"yung mesa galing sa kwan"* (that table from *kwan*).
Ano?	What?
KJ	Killjoy.
Aray!	Ouch!
Ha?	What? A Tagalog alternative to the English "I beg your pardon".
For a while	When asking to speak to a person on the phone, the receiver would say "For a while," instead of saying "Please hold".

dos & don'ts **in the PHILIPPINES**   103

Hand-carry	Instead of carry-on luggage.
Shades	Instead of sunglasses.
Boss/Brod	When signalling for the waiter.
D.O.M.	Dirty Old Man.
D.I.	Dance Instructor.
O.A.	Over-acting.
M.U.	Mutual understanding (usually in reference to a romantic couple who are close but not yet accorded the boyfriend-girlfriend status).
Bading	Gay; slang of *bakla*.
Cowboy	Rough & tough person.
Aircon	Short for airconditioning.
Ref	Short for refrigerator.

The respectful Pilipino

When addressing an older or more important person in Pilipino, *po*, meaning sir or ma'am, is added. *Opo* (yes, sir) replaces *oo* (yes), and *hindi po* (no, sir) is used instead of merely *hindi* (no).

Mang or *Manong* is the respectful way of addressing elderly men. Usually you add the first name of this respected individual such as *Mang* Jose or *Manong* Jose. For women, *Manang* is used.

DO address older and more important people with respect. Use *po*, *manong/manang* and "sir". It would be better to grant them higher status than to be considered impolite.

Business acquaintances are addressed by his or her family name such as Mr. Cruz or Ms. Cruz. Filipinos are conscious of the titles granted to them. A lawyer expects to be addressed as "Attorney" and a physician called "Doctor", and so on. Most politicians get a thrill of being called by their elected positions like "Governor" or "Mayor". It is only when they ask you to be less informal that you may call them by their first names.

Melodic tune

Filipinos tend to speak in a gentle, almost singsong manner. The sweet lyrical manner in which Pilipino and the other dialects are spoken have been applied to the English language, too. Only laughter is boisterous.

Publications

Nationwide - English language newspapers

There are a number of English language newspapers published in Manila. The three with the widest circulation are: *Philippine Daily Inquirer, Manila Bulletin,* and the *Philippine Star.*

DO note however, in some remote provinces these dailies arrive in the afternoon and cost more than the Manila prices. In remote areas, the previous day's edition is usually available. But often, local provincial newspapers (also in English) are sold in some cities outside Manila. Tabloids with attention-grabbing headlines are written in Tagalog. (Even if you can't understand it, the very graphic photos will surely catch your attention).

Magazines

International magazines such as *Time, Newsweek, Reader's Digest,* and *Asiaweek* are available in most magazine stands, bookstores, and convenience stores. Copies of the American edition of *Vogue, Glamour,* and *Cosmopolitan* are up-to-date. Older issues are sold at cheaper prices. Few copies of the European editions of magazines make their way to Filipino magazine shelves. *Cosmopolitan* and *Good Housekeeping* both have local editions for Filipina women written by a local staff and reasonably priced.

For Expats

There is a weekly newspaper published specially for expatriates and foreign visitors called *What's On* & *Expat - The Philippine Guide.* Free copies are distributed in hotels, restaurants, and museums. It has festival listings, travel news, business and local news and features.

Books

The bookstores in Manila are impressive. Best selling paperbacks in the United States usually make their way straight to local bookstores. There are also bookstores specialising in selling more expensive hard-to-find hardbound books and Filipino publications. It's often cheaper to buy paperbacks here than in many foreign cities.

MAINLY FOR MEN

Philippines

This section may appear blunt and drastic to male readers but the intention is to be realistic.

The typical Filipino guy

To some foreigners, Filipino men don't appear too masculine. The typical Filipino male, just like his female counterparts, values looking and smelling good. He is concerned with his attractiveness, having the right haircut and wearing stylish, well-pressed, clean clothes. Don't be deceived. Masculinity has high regard in this country.

Traditionally, males are expected to be the family breadwinner. In gratitude for providing their material needs, his wife and children treat him like royalty at home. He need not help in the household chores. However, parental roles are no longer as clear-cut, as many Filipina wives are now working to augment the family income.

Sometimes, the Filipino man is not just the king of one household, but several homes. Yes, it is common for the Filipino to have a mistress, but it's not acceptable for women to play around. Double standards? We think so. While the Catholic Church does not accept it, having a mistress is tolerated by society on condition that he can provide for his

108   dos & don'ts in the PHILIPPINES

family. Unfortunately, often times the poor wife, mistresses and offspring are not properly supported or loved. The Filipino male feels macho if he has several children from different women. Some politicians and actors are clear examples of this. The proof is the many families they secretly keep and the bewildering number of children who regularly announce they are the son or daughter of...

Another expression of the Filipino's manliness is the many nights spent with his *barkada* (peer group). During many rounds of gin or beer, they outdo each other by boasting of their achievements, especially in wooing the ladies.

Even with the playboy macho image of the Filipino, he is still expected to be a gentleman. He must open doors for women, help carry her parcels and bags, and keep her safe. In courtship, he does everything to win the heart of his timid and shy love. Traditionally, a suitor will serve her family by chopping wood and pumping water, in between serenading his ladylove under her window. She, on the other hand, gives him a hard time by pretending disinterest to test his devotion for her. These days, it is easier to woo a woman. He can win her heart through several dates at fancy restaurants, flowers and boxes of chocolates.

Foreigners may be baffled by the conflicting image of a macho man and a dependent son. Filipino society expects males to be good sons who assist their parents on the farm or in the family business. Unlike his western counterparts who become independent by their late teen years, the Filipino son continues to depend on his parents into his adult years. This Filipino male stays in his family house until he gets married. Some never leave, instead they bring their wives home to live with their parents. They do this as loving sons who care for their parent's needs in old age.

dos & don'ts in the PHILIPPINES   109

Some guidelines:

DON'T get drunk alone in public places. Always be in the company of trustworthy friends when you go drinking.

DON'T carry too much cash when you go out. When you pull out your wallet to pay for your drinks in a bar, many will calculate how much money you've got with you. If you are being followed, head for the police station, or report to the hotel staff.

DO go slow on local alcoholic drinks. Filipino males are heavy gin and beer drinkers. Take it easy, for what they can consume may be too much for you.

DO take caution when drinking with folks in the provinces. They can drink shots of their local potent drinks such as *Lambanog* (a coconut nectar brandy) and *Basi* (fermented sugar cane nectar) all night long, while they boast about personal accomplishments.

DO remain alert of pickpockets all the time especially if you appear tipsy. You'll be surprised at how skilled they are in getting wallets from your back pocket without you noticing it.

110   dos & don'ts **in the PHILIPPINES**

DON'T trust that pretty lass. She may appear like a young, innocent girl, but looks can be deceiving. Once you bring her to your room, she may drug you and get your cash.

DON'T think all sexy girls are female. Some men dress like women and often appear even more beautiful. Dressed in sexy outfits, they stand in dark corners and offer their services to male passers-by. Once inside the car, their Adam's apple or manly voice may give them away. If this happens, just pay up. It's safer and less trouble than getting them angry!

DO report all crimes to the police if you are a victim or a witness.

DON'T be intimate with a woman, unless she is engaged or married to you. The conservative Filipina has reservations about intimacy, touching and the like.

DON'T abuse little children. Our country has become a destination for foreign paedophiles. After many harrowing stories, the penalties for sexual abuse of children have rightfully become extremely harsh. Do this country a favour, respect children.

Be aware that interracial relationships are not common in the Philippines. Many locals are only used to seeing foreigners with sex workers, as was prevalent when U.S. forces were stationed here. Also be warned that some Filipinas are extremely attracted to foreigners, especially Americans. They believe marrying an American will give them a better life. That they will be able to realise their dream of living in the United States - the land of opportunity, the land of milk and honey.

DON'T be surprised when people stare at you when in the company of a young Filipina. Some may even make snide remarks such as prosti or *pok-pok* referring to your companion as a prostitute. Simply ignore it.

PUBLIC PLACES

Philippines

The visitor will be shocked to find he can never be alone. Filipinos will gladly accompany you anywhere as they can't imagine anybody wanting to be by themselves. Certainly, they always have company. They don't like eating alone or watching a movie alone. They always prefer to have somebody by their side be it a friend or relative. In fact the first question a Filipino asks when he bumps into someone in the mall, restaurant or anywhere else is *"sinong kasama mo?"* (who are you with?). This assumes that you are always with someone else. In a country that is overpopulated, the saying 'The more, the merrier!' is obviously taken to heart. So wherever you are, you're bound to find yourself amidst Filipinos.

DO maintain a pleasant voice. Keep your voice soft and calm. Admittedly, some Filipinos can get hot under the collar, but it doesn't pay to do so. Raising your voice makes you appear confrontational and may lead to a fight. By maintaining a soft and calm tone, Filipinos will be friendlier.

DON'T lose your temper. Keep your cool. What good is it to blow your top when things go wrong? Filipinos will be less sympathetic to you. If you get angry, they may find you threatening and gang up against you. So hold your temper at all cost.

DO line up. Filipinos are not as disciplined as the Japanese when falling into line. The good news is Filipinos are becoming better at it. Getting in the *jeepney* or buying a movie ticket you're more likely these days to find a semblance of a line. Of course, there are some people who are impatient and conveniently squeeze

themselves near the head of the queue. Get in line, some friendly Filipino may even strike a conversation with you while waiting.

DON'T walk barefoot. The tropical weather in the Philippines may entice you to walk around barefoot, but it's not advisable. The streets and ground are dirty. You are bound to get all sorts of infections and perhaps illnesses doing so. Use comfy sandals or slippers instead. Be aware though that slippers (thongs or flip-flops) are not allowed in some establishments like hotels, upmarket stores, and restaurants.

dos & don'ts **in the PHILIPPINES**

DO dress properly. With the tropical heat, naturally you would like to wear less. But one need not look sloppy to feel comfortable. Wear fashionable clothing made of light and cool fabrics. Be aware that *sandos* (tank tops) are not allowed in most restaurants. Also, refrain from wearing extravagant gems. They will definitely attract robbers to you.

DON'T display your money. Seems pretty obvious, huh? When making purchases or paying for public transportation, bring out only a small amount of cash. Seeing a thick wad of peso bills in your wallet will definitely catch the attention of scheming thieves.

DO be wary of over-friendly individuals. While most locals are friendly, watch out for those who are extra nice. They may have malicious motives.

DO avoid establishments with drunk Filipinos especially police or military men. They like to show off and play around with their guns, resulting in accidents. Alcohol and guns don't mix well together.

DON'T spit. Some tourists and locals spit in the streets. Not only is it an unpleasant sight, it's also unsanitary.

DON'T be overly sympathetic to beggars. When street children or beggars mob you, firmly say *Patawad po*! meaning "forgive me, sir!". Giving to one beggar would lead others to pester you until you give them, too. The government is trying to eradicate panhandling and by giving donations, you are probably indirectly feeding some drug syndicate or petty gangsters. If you want to help, give them food or donate to non-government organisations instead.

dos & don'ts **in the PHILIPPINES** 117

DO maintain your sense of humour. No matter how difficult the situation, the good-natured Filipino still manages to smile or crack a joke. When caught by the cops for speeding or when he misses the last bus, the Pinoy maintains his sense of humour. So when everything seems to go wrong while in the Philippines, smile - it will get better!

RENTALS

Philippines

Many visitors will rent transport to get them around the islands. This may range from cars, vans, motorcycles and mountain bikes to boats and jet skis. Some of these vehicles may be in tiptop shape while others are barely functioning. Always be alert when renting anything.

For cars/vans

Cars and vans can be rented from world wide companies like *Avis, Hertz* and *Budget*, which provide rescue assistance and third party insurance. For smaller automobile rental companies, check the telephone directory or classified ads in the newspapers. If you are wise enough not to fight it out on the streets with insane Manila drivers, hiring chauffeur driven vehicles is recommended. Some hotels have vehicles and drivers for hire, though they tend to be costly.

Car rental companies require:

1. Driver's License or International Driver's License. The driver's license from your home country will be honoured for ninety days. After that period, you must obtain a Philippine driver's license from the Land Transportation Office (LTO) Main Office in East Avenue, Quezon City.

2. Credit Card.

3. Passport or airline ticket (as an assurance you will return the vehicle), if you paid in cash.

4. Cash deposit. Some small establishments require a deposit which will be returned to you when you return the car.

5. The car returned with a full tank of fuel.

DO check the vehicle for any damage before you take possession of it. You don't want to be stuck in some remote place with a poor quality vehicle. Test drive it if you wish, especially if you are taking a long trip. Check the tires including the spare, the tools, the engine, the oil, etc. Some car rental companies have a checklist of damage to the car (scratches, missing hubcaps, and so on). If you do not check carefully, you may be charged for this existing damage when you return the vehicle.

DO clarify with the vehicle owner who will pay, should there be a mechanical breakdown that requires a hefty repair bill. He will argue with you, since the insurance, if any, will cover stolen cars or accidents only. A breakdown *per se* is not an accident.

DO study the rental rates. If you know you will be using the vehicle for a long period, ask for a special rate. Be aware that the rental rate does not include gasoline charges, tolls, and parking charges. Consider renting on weekdays instead of weekends to take advantage of special midweek discounts.

DO be aware that petrol is called gas in this country. So when you are lost and need to fill up your car, ask for the nearest gas station not petrol station. The good news is that most stations are full service stations. You need not pump your own gas, check your oil, and clean your windshield. A service attendant will do it for you.

For recreation vehicles

Popular beach destinations and resorts offer rental of various watersports equipment and bikes. These usually include jetski's, kayaks, canoes, speedboats, sail boats and windsurf boards. They can be rented by the hour or by the day. Spend a few minutes to ask resort employees how to properly use them. They will gladly teach you.

DO ask for the best rate. Use your charm and be friendly with the employees, they may throw in some bonuses like half-an-hour free use, or free rental of life jacket or snorkel.

DO wear a life jacket to be safe. Most rental shops charge for the use of life jackets. It's best not to scrimp on this; better to be safe than sorry.

DON'T be surprised when a boatman approaches you along the beach offering rental of his boat, for a fee of course. They will take you to sea for half a day or a full day of snorkelling or island hopping. Before committing yourself to one of these cunning men, ask around first. Another boatman may give you a better price. Be warned that they are very persistent. Once you show even just a tinge of interest, they will persevere until they finally convince you. Be equally persistent in bargaining for a cheaper rate.

Some useful Tagalog words

Can I hire	Puwede bang mag-arkila
- a car?	- ng kotse?
- a bike?	- ng bisikleta?
- a motorcycle?	- ng motorsiklo?
- a boat?	- ng bangka?
I need a car for one/three days?	Kailangan ko ng kotse para sa isang/tatlong araw?
How much is....?	Magkakano ang...?
- the deposit?	- deposito?
- the daily charge?	- bayad bawat araw?
- the cost of insurance?	- halaga ng insurance?
What documents do I need?	Anong mga documento ang kailangan ko?
Do you have a road map?	Mayroon ba kayong mapa?

Where's the nearest petrol station?	*Saan ang pinakamalapit na gasolinahan?*
How much per liter?	*Magkano ang isang litro?*
Fill it up.	*Punuin mo.*
Please check the ...	*Paki-check lang ang...*
Is there something wrong with the... ?	*Mayroon bang diperensya ang...?*
- tires	- *mga gulong/mga goma*
- water in the radiator	- *tubig sa* radiator
- oil	- *baterya*
- brakes	- *preno*
- carburetor	- *karburador*
- exhaust	- *tambutso*
- gear shift	- *kambyo*
- gas tank	- *tanke ng gasolina*
- steering wheel	- *manibela*

RESTAURANTS

Philippines

Dining at a restaurant can be very stressful and at times annoying for the visitor. Just when you are hungry, tired and sweaty, everything seems to go wrong with the meal. The dining experience at a restaurant may easily turn into a nightmare. Your waiter returns fifteen minutes later only to tell you your order is not available. Your order does not turn out as you expected. You wait an hour for your food. You are overcharged. But, dining in the Philippines need not be an unpleasant experience.

Knowing where to go and what to look out for is key. Plus, lots of patience!!

DO choose your restaurants with care.

Manila and popular tourist destinations like Cebu, Davao, Baguio, and Boracay have a wide variety of restaurants from fine dining and family restaurants to the fast-food chains - both American and Filipino. There is so much international cuisine, you'll be spoilt for choice: Filipino, Chinese, Japanese, Thai, Vietnamese, Indian, American, Italian... When you want something familiar, cheap, and quick, rely on the ever-dependable fast-food chains like *McDonald's, Burger King, Wendy's, KFC, Pizza Hut*, etc. and local fast-food dependables like *Jollibee, Chowking* and *Greenwich*. But don't miss out on one of the great joys of travelling - sampling different flavours of the local cuisine.

DO eat all the food taken from the buffet as some establishments charge more if you leave leftovers on your plate. So, get only what you can finish. You can return for seconds, anyway.

DO ask hotel staff or acquaintances where it is best to eat and what dishes to sample. Be specific what sort of food you want and how much you're prepared to spend. Filipinos will gladly point you to the direction of their favourite eateries. It would be a pity to leave the place without tasting its culinary best!

In the provinces, there are not too many international restaurants. Restaurants usually serve local fare. Since many bodies of water surround the Philippines, try the tasty seafood specialities: all sorts of fish, crab, squid, lobster, mussels and clams.

DO speak slowly and clearly. Even though most Filipinos understand English, they might get confused with your accent. Remember, Filipinos are embarrassed to clarify things and may just smile at you as if they understand every word. To be sure they got your order, ask your waiter or waitress to repeat it to you.

DO ask questions about the dishes. When you are not sure what the dish is, ask the waiter to describe it. The last thing you need is to be served something you didn't want in the first place.

Dishes are usually prepared to suit Filipino taste. Pasta sauces tend to be sweeter as Filipinos find Italian sauces too sour. Indian and Thai food tends to be less spicy as Filipinos can only tolerate

dos & don'ts **in the PHILIPPINES**

so much spice (except those from the Bicol region). Also ask how big the dish is. Most restaurants have big servings as Filipinos like to share the dishes, family-style.

DO explain any allergies or food preference explicitly to the waiter. If you are vegetarian, tell the waiter you cannot eat meat or animal fat in any shape or form. Some waiters pass off dishes without visible meat chunks as vegetarian. Only when sampling the dish does the diner realise it is made with meat stock.

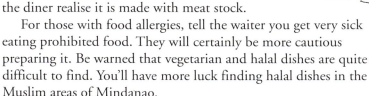

For those with food allergies, tell the waiter you get very sick eating prohibited food. They will certainly be more cautious preparing it. Be warned that vegetarian and halal dishes are quite difficult to find. You'll have more luck finding halal dishes in the Muslim areas of Mindanao.

"Captain", "Boss"

Filipinos tend to call waiters "Captain" or "Boss" to give significance to them and to be on their good side. It is also acceptable to call them "waiter". Waitresses are often referred to as "Miss!".

Asking for the bill

Filipinos have a peculiar way of asking for the bill. They call the waiter, raise their hands in the air with the fingers making a rectangle, and say "bill, please!", "*chit*, please" or "check, please." Oftentimes the silent language of

128   dos & don'ts **in the PHILIPPINES**

motioning a rectangle in the air is enough to be understood by the waiters.

Paying the Bill

In the Philippines, the one who invites others to a meal automatically pays the entire bill. Going dutch is not common and is an insult to the one who calls you for dinner. In cases where you casually have lunch or dinner with officemates or friends, you usually go dutch. So be careful when you invite a big group to dine with you, you may be forced to shoulder the cost of the meal. Fortunately, most restaurants accept major credit cards!

DO check the bill first

Sometimes your bill includes those items you subsequently cancelled when you decided to make a switch. It might also include items you never ordered, or ordered but never arrived. Or sometimes, drinks may be billed twice.

At the end of your bill, ten percent tax is usually added. Other restaurants, also add a ten percent service charge. If the bill is not clear, clarify with the waiter.

To tip or not to tip?

Tipping is not expected outside hotel restaurants and fine dining establishments, but any waiter would appreciate a small token like ten or twenty pesos. Unlike Americans who consistently give ten percent of the bill as a tip, Filipinos usually give less. Play it by ear. If service charge is included in the bill, a small amount will do. If you were extremely happy with the service, leave five percent or more depending on how generous you feel.

dos & don'ts **in the PHILIPPINES**   129

Useful Pilipino expressions

Table conversation

I'm hungry.	*Nagugutom ako.*
I'm thirsty.	*Nauuhaw ako.*
Can you recommend a good restaurant?	*Puwede ka bang magrikomenda ng isang mabuting restoran?*
Can you recommend a good but inexpensive restaurant?	*Puwede ka bang magrikomenda ng isang restoran na hindi masyadong mahal?*
I'd like to reserve a table for two.	*Gusto kong magpareserve ng lamesa para sa dalawa.*
Come at 7:30 pm.	*Darating kami ng a las siyete-medya ng gabi.*
May I have the menu please?	*Pahingi nga ng menu?*
Could we have a/an?	*Pahingi nga ng ...*
- spoon	- *kutsara*
- fork	- *tinidor*
- knife	- *kutsilyo*
- glass	- *baso*
- plate	- *plato*
- napkin	- *napkin/serbilyeta*
I'd like a/an/some...	*Gusto ko sana ng...*
- beer	- *beer/serbesa*
- bread	- *tinapay*
- butter	- *mantikilya*
- catsup	- *katsup*
- chicken	- *manok*
- coffee	- *kape*
- fish	- *isda*
- fruit	- *prutas*
- ice cream	- *ice cream/sorbetes*
- meat	- *karne*

- milk - *gatas*
- mineral water - *mineral water or tubig na nasa bote*

- mustard - *mustasa*
- pepper - *paminta*
- potatoes - *patatas*
- rice - *kanin*
- rolls - *tinapay*
- salad - *salad*
- salt - *asin*
- sandwich - *sanwits*
- soda (soft drinks) - *sopdrinks*
- soup - *sopas*
- sugar - *asukal*
- tea - *cha-a*
- vegetable - *gulay*
- vinegar - *suka*
- water (hot) - *mainit na tubig*
- water (cold) - *malamig na tubig*
- wine - *alak*

May I have another one? *Pahingi ng isa pa.*

Complaints

That's not what I ordered — *Hindi iyan ang inorder ko.*

I don't like this. — *Ayaw ko nito.*

I can't eat this. — *Hindi ito pwedeng makain.*

May I change this? — *Puwede ba itong palitan?*

The meat is …. — *Ang karne ay …*
- overcooked - *sobrang pagkaluto*
- underdone - *hilaw*
- too tough - *masyadong matigas*

This is too… — *Masyadong itong …*
- bitter - *mapait*
- salty - *maalat*

- sweet
- *matamis*

The food is cold. *Malamig na ang pagkaing ito.*

This isn't fresh. *Hindi ito sariwa.*

This is stale. *Luma na ito.*

Would you ask the head waiter/manager to come over? *Puwede mo bang tawagin yung head waiter/manager?*

Paying the bill

May I have the bill (check) please? *Akin na ang chit.*

Didn't you make a mistake? *Hindi ba kayo nagkamali?*

Is service charge included? *Kasama na ba dito ang service charge/tip?*

Do you accept credit cards? *Tumatanggap ba kayo ng credit card?*

Can I have the receipt? *Pahingi ng resibo.*

Thank you *Salamat.*

This tip is for you. *Ito'y para sa iyo.*

Keep the change. *Sa iyo na ang sukli.*

That was a very good meal. *Masarap ang pagkain.*

We enjoyed it. *Nagustuhan namin.*

We'll come again sometime. *Babalik ulit kami dito.*

SHOPPING

Philippines

Shopping is an exciting activity enjoyed immensely by tourists and Filipinos alike. The shopper may choose to go to the vast malls in the metropolis, or the small stores in the towns, or the seasonal bazaars throughout the city. There are many bargains to purchase: clothes, shoes, handicrafts and more. If you know the art of shopping in the Philippines, you can make your peso go a long way.

DO be aware of imitations and overruns. Brand name T-shirts, wallets, shoes, watches and other goods are sold at a fraction of the prices abroad. Wow, what a bargain! Watch out, they are just imitations or some export overruns (slightly damaged goods). But if you check carefully, you will be rewarded to find some good quality items. If you just want a cheap shirt then the imitation from bazaars is fine. If you want the real thing, head for the big department stores.

DO be wary of pickpockets in bazaars. Bazaars (in Divisoria, Baclaran and Greenhills) may be great for finding cheap imitations and export overruns. But keep your eye on your wallet or your handbags because there are many pickpockets ready to victimise shoppers. While you are busy haggling for lower prices, they quickly slash your bag or grab your wallet. Make sure your bags are zipped up or properly closed. Since these places are too crowded, it is likely that your toes will be stepped on a couple of times. If you are wearing sandals, your poor toenails might die!

DO purchase export quality Philippine products. Take advantage of the beautifully crafted handicrafts, furniture, bags, hats, baskets, embroidery, hand woven textiles and fresh fruit products the Philippines is known for. These items cost a fortune once they are exported.

DO haggle for lower prices. As a rule, always haggle for a lower price except in department stores and boutiques. Storekeepers tend to quote tourists higher prices. When the storekeeper refuses to budge, pretend not to be interested anymore. Act as if you are leaving, you'll soon get the price you want.

When you haggle, ask for a big discount. Say the shirt is P300, ask for P150. The shopkeeper will probably say P250, until you finally agree on P200. There are no set rules. Start low because you can be sure the shopkeeper will haggle for a higher price anyway.

DO shop early to get discounts. In the Philippines, the early bird gets not the worm, but a bargain. Shopkeepers believe that the first customer brings in luck for the day. So shopkeepers give a lower price to early shoppers. Once the shopkeeper receives the money from the first purchaser, she brushes it on all her goods to spread good luck. It is deemed unlucky when the first people making inquiries do not make a purchase. It is better to sell the product at a lower price to the first customer, than to have bad luck or no customers for the rest of the day. So, shop early, you may be the lucky customer of many vendors!

DO try to keep an eye on your credit card all the time. If possible, request for it to be endorsed in front of you, not in the backroom where the operator is out of sight for a long time. If this happens, suspect some foul play.

dos & don'ts **in the PHILIPPINES** 135

DON'T be offended when the vendor calls you *barat* meaning haggler. It means you have already mastered the art of shopping Pinoy-style

Some useful words & expressions

Where's the nearest...?	*Nasaan ang pinakamalapit na...?*
- antique shop	- *tindahan ng mga antik*
- bakery shop	- *panaderia/bakery*
- bank	- *bangko*
- barber shop	- *barberia/pagupitan*
- barong tagalog store	- *tindahan ng barong*
- beauty salon	- *beauty parlour/ beauty salon*
- bookstore	- *tindahan ng libro*
- butcher's shop	- *bilihan ng karne*
- camera shop	- *bilihan ng film*
- dress shop	- *modista*
- drugstore	- *botika*
- fish market	- *bilihan ng isda sa palengke*
- flea market	- *tiangge/ bilihan ng segunda mano*
- florist	- *bilihan ng bulaklak*
- fruit market	- *bilihan ng prutas sa palengke*
- garments store	- *bilihan ng tela*
- green grocer	- *bilihan ng gulay*
- jewellery store	- *tindahan ng mga alahas*
- market	- *palengke*
- shoe store	- *tindahan ng sapatos*
- tailor	- *sastre*
- watch store	- *bilihan at pagawaan ng relo*
- wine store	- *tindahan ng alak*
I want....	*Gusto ko...*
Can you show me some...?	*Puwede mo ba akong pakitaan....?*
Do you sell....?	*Nagtitinda ba kayo ng...?*
I'd like to buy...	*Gusto kong bumuli ng...*
Do you have any... ?	*Mayroon ba kayong ...?*
Where's the ..... department?	*Nasaan ang bilihan ng...?*
That one!	*Iyan!*
How much?	*Magkano?*
How much is this?	*Magkano ito?*
I'll take it.	*Kukunin ko na 'yan.*
May I have a shopping bag please?	*Puwede bang makahingi ng supot/plastic bag?*

SUPERSTITIOUS BELIEFS & FOLK PRACTICES

Philippines

Before the Spaniards introduced Christianity to the Philippines, Filipinos believed in spirits, fairies, witches, dwarfs, and elves. Today, even with strong Catholic faith, most Filipinos still believe in superstitions. Pinoys still avoid unlucky numbers, follow a particular order and harmony of objects, fear witches, dwarfs and even believe offering eggs can stop the rain! Though Filipinos realise that some of these beliefs are ridiculous and have no logical explanations, they still continue to follow them. Read the twelve popular superstitions, supernatural beings, and strange practices widely followed and believed throughout the islands. Listing thirteen superstitions may be unlucky, so we stopped at twelve. You'll probably encounter more as you stay longer in the country.

Feng Shui

Feng Shui is a Chinese belief in the proper arrangement of things to create harmony. Incorrect arrangement of objects may cause a household or business misfortune. Gaining popularity outside the Chinese community in the past few years, architects now consult *Feng Shui* experts to be assured no bad fortune will be caused by their designs.

Oro, Plata, Mata

Another belief that must be considered in the construction of houses and buildings is the number of steps in the stairs. Each step corresponds to *Oro* (gold), *Plata* (Silver), or *Mata* (death). Should the last step fall on *Oro* or *Plata*, this is considered lucky for the tenants. However, the last step ending in *Mata* (death) is deemed unlucky.

Tinutumbok

A street that leads right smack to a house, or *tinutumbok*, is said to be unlucky. Filipinos have attributed failed marriages, bankruptcy, and poor businesses to residing in a house *na tinutumbok*. Keep this in mind when renting or buying a house.

Friday the 13th

Just like Westerners, Filipinos are fearful when the 13th day of the month falls on a Friday. Strange occurrences and bad luck are said to abound on this fatal day.

Bed facing the door

Never position your bed facing the door. Doing so will result in an early exit from this world.

Kulam

Sudden headaches, excruciating stomach pain, or strange blotches on the skin without a logical origin are said to be results of a *kulam*. There is widespread belief that some individuals called *mangkukulam* have special power to cause illness or death by casting spells. The victim must be treated not by a physician, but by a traditional healer who can counteract sorcery.

Aswang & manananangal

An *aswang* is a vampire believed to prey upon his fellow men, especially children, the sick, the recently bereaved and pregnant women. This evil creature may take the

dos & don'ts in the PHILIPPINES

form of animals such as a pig or a dog to harm its chosen victim. His female counterpart is the *manananggal*, a female vampire who can disengage the top half of her body and fly at night to the beds of unsuspecting men. Sprinkling salt on the severed half torso will slay this wicked creature. Watch out, your lovely date may secretly be a *manananggal*!

Nuno sa punso

While trekking in the mountains, Pinoys would whisper *tabi, tabi!* (move aside, move aside). This is a friendly reminder to the *nuno sa punso* or the tiny old man who dwells on an anthill. You should not trespass or worse destroy anthills as this little fellow may cause you bad health or ill fortune.

Tabi, tabi! is also used to ask permission from other spirits of the forest to pass through their dwelling places. Be a polite guest of the mountain and forest spirits. It's just like saying "Excuse Me!" when you trespass on someone's property.

Gayuma or love potion

Filipinos are passionate lovers. When their object of desire does not return their love, they resort to *gayuma* or love potions made of a mixture of roots, bark, stones and seeds. So when a person immediately becomes attracted to an unlikely match or is deeply lovesick, it's probably *gayuma* at work. If you want to improve your love life, put some helpless person under your love spell. But there is no assurance it will last!

Amulet or *Anting-anting*

Amulets or *anting-antings* are said to ward off harm and evil. These special charms also provide supernatural powers. Certain tree branches may cause illness or death on your enemies and a special leaf may bring your desired man/woman to fall in love with you. Quite powerful, huh? Traditionally, these amulets came from mountainous forest areas. But today a variety of amulets with various powers are now sold in Quiapo, a busy district of Manila. The belief that these little icons bring fertility, prosperity, or make you invincible has made them very popular among Filipinos.

Eggs to stop the rain!

Scared it might rain at your garden party or beach outing? Offer some eggs to Santa Clara! For many years now, Filipinos have been sending eggs to the Sisters of Saint Clare with a request to pray for clear skies. Of course, there are no guarantees. But many attest it works.

dos & don'ts **in the PHILIPPINES**

It's bad to point!

DON'T point. While it is universally known to be impolite to point at people, Filipinos refrain from pointing at objects too. Why? While you may be pointing in the direction of the object, you may be pointing to a spirit. This may offend the spirit and harm you. So think twice before you aim your forefinger in a certain direction.

SWIMMING, SCUBA DIVING & SNORKELLING

Philippines

In an archipelago of 7,107 islands with gorgeous beaches, it is very enticing to take a dip. But before you dive in, follow the advice in this chapter. Some may seem very basic, but it's best not to take our wise words for granted.

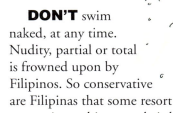

DON'T swim naked, at any time. Nudity, partial or total is frowned upon by Filipinos. So conservative are Filipinas that some resort to wearing a shirt over their bathing suit when swimming. Unlike Westerners who prefer two-piece suits, Filipinas wear less revealing one-piece suits.

If you are seen swimming naked, you're bound to attract a crowd. They will think you are insane or simply flirting with trouble. In beaches with lots of people, you will definitely be talked about. In remote places, women could be harassed or even raped. And if you are harmed, locals will not sympathise with you. They will say you are asking for it. Wear a two-piece suit if you wish, but never swim naked.

DON'T sunbathe topless. Just like swimming naked, a topless woman invites stares and trouble! Again, this woman is seen as cheap and vulgar.

DO protect yourself from the sun. Apply sunblock lotion liberally. The heat is intense in this country, especially during the

144   dos & don'ts **in the PHILIPPINES**

summer months (mid-March to May). Stay in the shade from noon to 2pm when the sun's rays are intense. You may burn easily or worse, suffer heat stroke. Use UV-protected shades for your eyes and a hat for your scalp as well. Of course, battle dehydration by replenishing lost fluids. Drink lots of water.

The sea

With thousands of islands come thousands of stretches of golden sand. There are many inviting beaches, but not all are great for swimming.

DO swim from a beach near a resort, to be safe. Some beaches are secluded for a reason - they are not safe for swimming. Don't be deceived! While the ocean may look calm and enticing, below could be dangerous undertow areas with treacherous currents.

DON'T swim alone. Beaches in the Philippines do not have warning signs for risky areas. It is best to have swimming companions in case you get into difficulties. If you are not a good swimmer, watch out. Some shallow areas become deep without warning.

DO watch out for rocks or corals. Many beaches are ideal for diving and snorkelling. These places may have the most colourful and vibrant corals, yet they can give you a nasty cut. You should also look out for sea urchins and jellyfish which can inflict excruciating pain. Wear aqua socks to protect your feet.

dos & don'ts in the PHILIPPINES

DON'T leave your valuables unattended on the shore. There are many vendors or fellow beach-goers that may be tempted to steal your things. Don't tempt fate.

DON'T touch the corals or take them home as a souvenir. These are homes to fish and other creatures of the sea. Just appreciate their beauty and colours. If you take them with you, years from now there will be no more sea life to return to.

DON'T buy sea shells. Yes, the beach vendors need your money but sea creatures need their homes too. By buying shells you are contributing to the depletion of species.

DON'T leave your garbage on the seashore. Take your candy wrappers or cans of soda back with you to your hotel. Dispose of them properly, especially non-biodegradable products like plastics.

Other places

DO remember that the cool surface of a waterfall pool may conceal a sharp boulder just where you think it's a good diving spot. Unfortunately, there are no warning signs.

DON'T answer the call of nature or wash your dirty dishes in a running stream (or any water for that matter), as villagers downstream depend on these waters for almost everything: for cooking, washing the clothes, even for drinking.

Scuba diving

The Philippines boasts more dive sites than any other country in the world. Most guidebooks identify dive sites or you may call the Philippine Commission on Sports and Scuba Diving (PCSSD) in Manila at 524-3735/525-4413.

DO bring your C-card and logbook. Philippine law requires these from anyone who rents equipment or hires guides.

DO bring your own scuba gear especially your own wet suit for that perfect fit. If you don't, no need to worry as most dive resorts have masks, fins, booties, weights, BCD's, tanks and regulators to rent at affordable prices.

DON'T dive alone. Always have a dive buddy. It's best to dive with a group of certified divers along with a dive master. The dive master will bring you to the best diving spots in the area and is prepared for any problem. It is not advisable to rely on the local boatmen who claim to be familiar with the good dive spots.

TOURING & TREKKING

Philippines

There is so much to see in the Philippines: gorgeous beaches, stunning sunsets, quaint towns, awesome historic churches, mountains and volcanoes, exotic flora and fauna, and a whole lot more. With ample preparation, you will find a Pinoy adventure to suit your taste and your budget.

DO invest in a comprehensive guidebook to discover the attractions, places to stay, where to dine and how to get to your destination. The nation's dailies also have regular travel features.

DO surf the web for a wealth of information about airline and resort rates, festival listings, even first hand experiences of recent visitors.

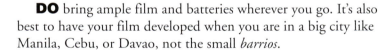

DO bring ample film and batteries wherever you go. It's also best to have your film developed when you are in a big city like Manila, Cebu, or Davao, not the small *barrios*.

Conducted tours

DO call the Travel Agencies listed in the Yellow Pages. Also check the calendar listings in the newspapers for upcoming tours. You'll find many, from the mundane to the specific like a tour of churches, a tour of particular towns and festivals, even nature treks.

Manila drivers, no, drivers throughout the country, swerve at heartstopping speed, stop without warning, squeeze their vehicles between huge buses, and perennially change lanes without signalling. Yes, it is a nightmare! The situation is even worse with the bad roads and endless road repairs and construction work. Some roads in the provinces are not well paved and if you're riding a diesel powered vehicle both can combine to give you the nauseous feelings that your insides have been rearranged.

DO gulp down a couple of travel sickness pills beforehand if you are a sensitive passenger.

DO be wary of tour guides who insist on bringing you to certain shops. They are definitely getting commissions on everything you buy. And you will not be getting the bargains or the choice you deserve.

DO ask for the details of the tour and what is and is not included in the package, like meals and snacks. Also, knowing the details of your tour will enable you to dress properly for the trip.

Personal sight-seeing

Often times, it is better to explore the country on your own. There are many places which are easily accessible from Manila by land, air or sea. Taking on this adventure is best if
1) you are young, strong and have a companion;
2) you know for sure you can take the rough and tough aspects of

any tropical country road or forest; 3) you are prepared for anything! With some preparation and careful planning, personal sight-seeing can be enjoyable. Just don't be too confident. Remember, you must be fully alert all the time and accept full responsibility for any mishap. Backpackers, especially females, should be extremely careful.

DO carefully consider whether to rent a car or take public transport to your destination. Once there, is it easy to get around? It may be effortless to get there by bus, plane or boat, but once you've arrived, suppose there are no *jeepneys* or tricycles to take you around?

DON'T forget to find out the time of the last bus/taxi/boat if you are planning a one-day trip.

DO not camp anywhere you like just because you have a sleeping bag or tent. Some places may be home to dangerous animals, like snakes. While others are privately owned and not welcoming of campers. Do ask around before setting up your tent.

DO be ready for sudden rainfall any time of the year. Though June to October is typhoon season, storms may hit as late as November. Always check first the radio, TV, or the web for weather forecasts. Typhoons may immediately cause floods (due to poor drainage systems) and disable road transport. It is best not to travel during this time as you would most likely be stranded. Land, air, and sea transport are cancelled during strong typhoons.

DO bring an umbrella and a raincoat when you travel.

DO have insect repellent with you all the time. For some reason, mosquitoes like foreigners more than locals. Or maybe, locals tend to ignore the bites.

Insect bites are not only irritating and itchy, but also harmful. Serious tropical diseases like malaria are spread by mosquitoes. Its symptoms are headaches, fever, chills, sweating which may subside and recur. Without treatment, malaria may develop some serious and potentially fatal effects. So if you are travelling to Palawan or Mindanao, where malaria is more widespread than in other parts of the country, it is extremely important to take malarial prophylactics. They have to be taken for a period of time before you depart and after you return. Consult your doctor.

DO bring emergency medicines with you. Pharmacies in the provinces may not carry the medicine you need. Purchase your medicines before you leave your home country or before leaving Manila.

DO carry small bills. While carrying P1,000 bills seems easier, most vendors, tricycle, taxi, and jeepney drivers don't have change for big denominations. Cash is advisable as traveller's cheques and credit cards are not honoured in smaller establishments outside the cities.

dos & don'ts **in the PHILIPPINES**

Trekking

DO check the weather forecast before you set out for a hike. Wet and slippery conditions are dangerous. You can easily get lost when trails disappear or turn into streams.

DO investigate the security situation in the area where you intend to hike. The Philippines is generally safe but from time to time local conditions can be fractious. Consult your embassy for their travel advisory.

DON'T wear military-style clothing.

DO inform the people in your hotel and local officials (*Barangay Captain*) in the area of your hike, your plans and the duration of your trip.

DO bring a photocopy of your ID with a phone number of the person to contact in case of an emergency. Leave your driver's license, passport and other important ID's in the hotel safe.

DON'T trek alone. It is best to be with a group led by an experienced trekker or local guide. Besides, joining a group means more people to split the load with.

DON'T touch any wild plant or flower. Some may appear beautiful but are in fact, poisonous! Experienced mountaineers advise wearing gloves when climbing a mountain, so you can freely cling to sturdy tree trunks and vines.

DON'T swim in a river unless you are told it is safe.

DON'T pull a leach from your skin because part of it is likely to remain attached to you turning the wound septic. Instead, sprinkle salt on it, or light a match under the end that is wiggling about. In both cases the leach will drop off.

DO wear comfortable hiking shoes. It is quite difficult to negotiate a slippery mountain while wearing unsuitable sandals.

DO bring suitable hiking gear: the lightweight tent, some cooking utensils, lots of drinking water, canned food, a blanket or sleeping bag, a flashlight. Keep equipment down to essentials. Carrying extra pounds while climbing a mountain is not fun. The less you have to carry, the better.

DON'T drink alcohol when you climb. While it may seem enticing to drink under the stars at night, alcohol will further dehydrate you. You won't be in the best shape for the strenuous activities to get you down the mountain the next day.

DON'T leave your garbage behind. Whatever you take up to the mountain,

dos & don'ts in the PHILIPPINES

you must bring down with you. Even if it is tempting to leave empty cans or bottles to lighten your load, don't do it. As a responsible hiker, you must respect the environment.

DON'T hitchhike, as you are inviting trouble.

DON'T take the unbeaten path as it is not a path at all. In mountains, follow only well used paths.

DO take note that some mountains are home to indigenous tribes or religious cults. Mount Banahaw, about four hours north of Manila, is a favourite of *spiritistas*. They believe this mountain has supernatural powers. Always obtain information about mountains and trekking routes before you set off. Having a local guide climb with you is helpful and essential.

TRAVELLING & GETTING AROUND

Philippines

The experience of travelling can be quite overwhelming. It is easy for tourists to fall into some kind of trap, making the trip more disappointing than pleasurable.

DO be suspicious of free offers, voluntary guides, and unsolicited recommendations to shops. Reason: nobody does anything for free. Many scams abound.

This starts upon arriving at the airport. Some very friendly and helpful men will voluntarily carry your luggage to your car. They will be expecting you to tip them, even if you did not ask for their service. Immediately, say "NO!"

DO reject all offers of free refreshment and food. You might end up asleep!

DO bring *baon*. Whether they are going on a long trip or merely commuting to the office, Filipinos bring some food or *baon*. It can be a sandwich or a rice meal. A bottle of mineral water to quench your thirst along the way is always handy.

DO count your change at all counters, be it currency booths, ticketing windows at bus terminals, movie houses, or food centres. Many cashiers are good at making mistakes to their advantage.

DO bring a roll of toilet paper or tissue paper. This will come in handy, especially since most public rest rooms don't come equipped with it.

Airplanes

Airports in the Philippines, especially the Ninoy Aquino International Airport in Manila, tend to be bursting with humanity. Visitors get overwhelmed and swamped with the number of people who greet their returning relatives or friends. And there are many others including porters, policemen and security guards, taxi and hotel representatives crowding the exits. Departure is less disordered, but several family members send off their loved ones with tears in their eyes. So prepare for one big chaotic experience.

DO call the airline to confirm your international flight at least 48 hours prior to departure.

DO plan to be at the airport three hours before departure for an international flight. With the terrible traffic in Manila, also factor in travel time to the airport. It usually takes an hour to check-in, since the line for economy passengers is always long.

DO arrive at the airport at least 45 minutes before your domestic flight. Many passengers miss their plane due to the horrendous traffic, so they end up waiting as 'chance passengers' for the next flight. Unfortunately, some cities have only one flight a day. If you purchased your discounted ticket at the airlines' promotion price (where the ticket must be paid for a certain number of days prior to your departure), you will have to pay an additional fee when you request to be booked on a flight later in the day.

DO make seat reservations when you purchase your ticket, so you are assured of your preferred window or aisle seat.

DON'T bring huge hand-carried pieces of luggage. You are allowed two pieces which will fit the overhead cabin or below the seat in front of you. Filipinos are notorious for passing off gigantic bags as hand-carried pieces to prevent paying the excess baggage rates.

DON'T be surprised at the number of boxes Filipinos bring with them. They are called *Balikbayan* boxes (*Balikbayan* is the person returning to his home country). These huge brown boxes contain everything purchased during the Pinoy's vacation, including the necessary gifts for friends and relatives.

For scuba divers, golf enthusiasts & bowlers

Be aware that PAL (Philippine Airlines) gives a special baggage allowance for sports enthusiasts on their domestic and international flights. An additional 15 to 30 kilos baggage allowance is granted, depending on the sport. They must first obtain the "Flying Sportsmen" ID card at any PAL sales & ticketing offices. Simply present this card upon check-in at the airport and the special baggage allowance is granted. No need to worry about paying excess baggage for those heavy golf clubs, scuba gear or bowling balls.

Buses

There are airconditioned and non-airconditioned buses that ply the major routes and highways in Metro Manila. Signs hanging on the windshield show the bus's destination: bold letters point the first and last stops, smaller ones the stops along the route. Simply get in the bus and find a seat. The conductor goes around to collect the fare giving you a ticket in return. Keep it until you get off the bus. Street vendors peddling gum, cigarettes, candy, and newspapers hop on and off the non-airconditioned buses to sell their wares to passengers. Bus companies operate routes to provinces north and south of Manila. This is probably the most convenient and affordable way to see the countryside. Go to the bus terminals in Metro Manila for your ticket.

Airconditioned buses bound for the provinces are equipped with reclining chairs and luggage racks. Some even have a TV and VCR to provide entertainment on long trips. Passengers are left in suspense when they get off the bus before the movie ends. Others gladly get off at their destination rather than endure more hours in a bus with closed curtains, loud music, and trashy movies. A mini-toilet is also an added feature on some airconditioned buses.

In the provinces, there are smaller non-airconditioned buses, which make many stops along the way. These buses connect nearby towns and cities. Often overcrowded with lots of

dos & don'ts in the PHILIPPINES

passengers and piled high with boxes of produce, don't be surprised to find yourself looking into the beady eyes of a live chicken. Be stoic! The poor chicken is just enjoying his last few breaths before he is given as a gift and cooked for dinner.

DO give up your seat for that old woman. While it may inconvenience you to stand up during the bus ride, that old lady will really appreciate your thoughtful gesture. Be a gentleman.

DO note that most buses are not equipped with rest rooms. On long trips, they make several quick stops to allow customers to relieve themselves in public rest rooms or to grab a snack. If you have amazing bladder control, hold it until you get to your destination. Otherwise, hold your breath before using these public toilets.

DO arrive at the bus station at least an hour early. Immediately buy your ticket and board the bus to be assured a seat.

Trains

A cheap, but not necessarily easy way to get around the Metro Manila is the LRT (short for Light Rail Transit). A flat rate is charged for the token for the LRT to take you to any of the 18 stops from Caloocan to Baclaran. It operates from 5:30am to 9:30pm daily.

DON'T bring bulky loads as the LRT tends to be packed full. Taking the train to the countryside is not common practice. The PNR (Philippine National Railways) travels southbound from Manila to Bicol and northbound to San Fernando, La Union. If you don't mind travelling by slow and uncomfortable means, go to the Tutuban Station in Tondo to start your adventure.

Jeepney - the king of the road

If there is an unofficial symbol by which the Philippines is known all around the world, it is probably the *jeepney*. Its bright colours and gaudy decorations will surely grab your attention. If that doesn't work, the quick movements and stops wildly orchestrated by the *jeepney* driver will do the trick. Yes, this fancy contraption called the *jeepney* has earned its title as 'King of the Road.'

Its origin is in surplus US Army jeeps which were imaginatively converted into a practical mode of transportation. The body was lengthened to accommodate two long seats facing each other to seat ten or more passengers. And then came the hallmarks of the *jeepney*, each unique and each determining its personality. They are decorated inside and out with eye catching accessories like nickel horses planted on the hood, splashes of colour painted all over, an image of the Santo Niño with a

dos & don'ts **in the PHILIPPINES**   163

flickering light near the driver, *sampaguita* flower garlands hanging on the rear view mirror, witty sayings displayed on the dashboard.

The wide windows allow air to circulate freely into the *jeepney*. On rainy days, the rolled plastic is pulled down to keep the commuters dry. Some are like mobile discos with the driver's favourite songs blaring from speakers.

There is no typical *jeepney*. Each one reflects the creativity of its owner. What is the same is the fare: a flat rate is observed by all *jeepney* drivers in the city.

Riding the *jeepney* must be experienced. Before you stop one that catches your fancy, read the destinations painted outside the jeep. Once you find one going in your direction, stop it and hop in. The front seats next to the driver are much coveted and usually taken. Climb in the rear and find a spot among the rest of the dozen or so passengers. Grasp the handrail on the ceiling so you won't be thrown off: *jeepneys* move on even if passengers are barely seated. Once you've regained your composure, pay the fare by extending your hand to the driver and say *"Mama, bayad po."* To get off, say *"para po"* or tap the ceiling to announce you are getting off.

The Anatomy of a *Jeepney*

- mud guards with witty quotations
- the wheel outside the jeep hanging near the driver's left arm
- the driver with his "Good Morning!" towel hanging around his neck
- the passengers
- *sabit* (a freeloader at the rear door railings of one of the overloaded *jeepneys* clinging on to dear life as it speeds away)
- the horses in front
- the lights and decoration inside: God Bless Our Trip
- the *Santo Niño* near the driver
- the *Sampaguita,* the coins
- the colourful design outside
- the stops displayed on the side

dos & don'ts **in the PHILIPPINES**   165

DO bring small change when riding the *jeepney*.

DON'T wear fancy jewellery. Robbers have no qualms about snatching a necklace or bracelet from helpless passengers in broad daylight.

DO familiarise yourself with the routes of the *jeepney*. When you are not sure, ask the *jeepney* driver before hopping in.

DON'T hang on to the rear of the *jeepney*. Vendors and some local commuters have mastered hanging on without falling off. But for foreigners this is not recommended! We want you to leave our country as you came in, not in a coffin.

Tricycles & pedicabs

Too lazy to walk short distances? Pinoys have a solution. Take the tricycle. A small cab made of iron sheets is attached to the side of a motorcycle enabling three or four passengers to ride with the driver.

The Pedicab is just like the tricycle, the only difference is the driver has to pedal his bicycle to get you around. These small and humble modes of transportation are quite popular in the provinces. The commuter is transported from his or her doorstep to their destination for just a few pesos.

Cars

There are too many cars in Manila's streets today. To ease traffic problems, a scheme has been imposed banning cars in Metro Manila one day every week. Those with number plates ending in 1 and 2 are banned from 7 am to 7 pm on Mondays, plate numbers ending in 3 and 4 on Tuesdays,

5 and 6 on Wednesdays, 7 and 8 on Thursdays, and 9 and 0 on Fridays. On Saturdays from 9:30 am to 2:30 pm plates ending in odd numbers are banned from some streets and from 2:30 pm to 7:30 pm, plates ending in even numbers are banned from the some main roads. A hassle for motorists but it has eased the traffic considerably.

DO lock your car all the time. Car thefts are rampant in the city. No matter how old your car is, thieves are creative enough to find a use for it. Side mirrors, car radio, hub caps are popularly stolen. They probably end up in the second hand parts business. In fact you could end up buying the very same part stolen from your car!

dos & don'ts **in the PHILIPPINES**   167

DO not leave valuables in the car. These too will be stolen. There are many street children on the streets of Manila. Some sell *sampaguita leis*, cigarettes, gum or candy to motorists while the light is red at the traffic intersections. Other kids beg from motorists. Some kids are *bantay's*. As you park your car, they will ask if they can watch it for you. Technically, this is supposed to ensure your car's safety. When you return, you hand them a few pesos. As everybody knows, in reality your car was not safer with the kid watching it. But it is still best to play along with this charade. The few pesos you give ensure they will not scratch or damage your car.

Taxis

DO insist metered taxis turn on the meter as you get in. Often, drivers conveniently forget to turn off the previous fare. If the driver refuses to turn the meter on, get out and pay nothing, for it means he will overcharge you at the end of the journey. Be aware that the meter remains on even while you and the driver get stuck in a traffic jam.

DO negotiate the fixed fare to your destination with the airport shuttle representatives stationed right outside the airport. Drivers sometimes take advantage of the uninformed, jetlagged, weary foreigners and overcharge them.

Boats

Getting from one island to another will sooner or later require riding some type of boat. There are ships, ferries, and smaller boats to serve you. Manila is the jump-off point to major provinces and cities, while Cebu is the secondary link between Visayas and Mindanao. Inter-island ships have a variety of accommodation to suit your budget from the luxurious cabin to a basic cot. It is recommended to make reservations a day or two before departure.

Ferryboats service medium to large outlying islands. Passengers sit on deck chairs for half an hour to two hours. Pump boats and *bancas* are motorised and unmotorised boats that connect nearby islands to each other. Boatmen fill up the boat with passengers before beginning the trip.

This may seem obvious to most, but a good reminder anyway: don't ride a boat when it is raining, or worse when a typhoon is forecast. Several ferries have sunk due to storms and overloading. So be very careful. Patronise reputable shipping lines only.

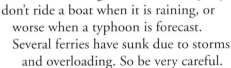

DON'T be mesmerised by cheap fares. The cheaper they are the more you could be risking your life.

dos & don'ts in the PHILIPPINES   169

Some useful Tagalog phrases

Where does this road lead?	*Saan patungo ang kalsadang ito?*
Is this the way to ...?	*Ito ba ang daan patungo sa...?*
Do you know the way to....?	*Alam mo ba ang daan patungo sa...?*
Where may I park?	*Saan ako puwedeng pumarada?*
I feel seasick.	*Ako'y nahihilo at nasusuka.*
Where will the boat stop?	*Saan titigil ang barko?*
Where's the airline ticketing airline?	*Saan ang ticketing office ng office?*
I've lost my ticket.	*Nawala ang aking ticket.*
I want to make a reservation for flight...	*Gusto kong magpareserba sa flight...*
When is the next flight to...?	*Kailan ang susunod na flight papuntang ... ?*
I'd like to cancel my flight to...	*Gusto kong i-cancel ang aking flight sa...*
Can you reschedule my flight to...?	*Puwede bang i-reschedule ang aking flight sa...?*
I'd like a change of destination.	*Gusto kong magbago ng destination.*

VISITING THE SICK

Philippines

Emphasized many times in this book, Filipinos do everything together. Just like married couples, Pinoys are together "in sickness and in health". Friends and relatives commiserate with and comfort the sick. If you have a sick Filipino friend in hospital, you must visit.

The sick person's room becomes the backdrop for a gathering of friends and relatives. With the patient resting in bed, family and friends drop by to show concern and support. Flowers and fruit are given to cheer up their ailing friend or relative. Following the same rules for hospitality in Filipino homes, refreshments are offered to visitors.

One relative or friend stays with the patient throughout the night to attend to his or her needs. This explains why an extra bed is found in hospital rooms in the Philippines. Women who have just given birth experience this special attention too.

MAINLY FOR WOMEN

Philippines

Filipinos are fascinated and intrigued by foreigners, especially women. Men and women in the Philippines find themselves staring in admiration at blonde Caucasian lady visitors. If that's exactly what you are, and if you don't want to attract more attention to yourself, read about the typical Filipina and the proper way for women to behave in the islands.

Dalagang Pilipina

The young Filipina lass or the *dalagang Pilipina* is expected to be demure, shy and loyal to the end. Traditionally, a single Filipina must be pure and chaste, clean in body, free from make-up, a non-smoker, dainty at all times, good at domestic chores, equipped with her hanky, *pamaypay* (fan), and rosary, and of course, must be God fearing. Even with this rather feminine expectation of women, Filipinas have much power in society. In fact, women enjoy equality with men in many areas such as business and careers.

Women have excelled in many fields. The topnotcher in the Philippine Military Academy was a woman. The most notable lawyers and doctors are women. The senator who obtained the highest number of votes was a woman; even the CEO's of several multinational companies are women. This comes as no surprise, as women have consistently made their mark in Philippine history. Corazon Aquino, the famed first Filipina president who successfully succeeded a twenty-year dictatorship, is an excellent example. One Filipina made big news all over the world, even landing her name in the Guinness Book of World Records.

Unfortunately, her achievement of amassing thousands of shoes is not too impressive. Yes, we're talking about Imelda Marcos. Filipina women are expected to undergo sacrifices for their loved ones, especially for their children. This cultural expectation has driven many Filipinas to work as domestic helpers and nurses abroad. They may be away for years at a time just to provide a better life for their children.

The typical Filipina

- is hardworking, whether she is a professional, a teacher or a market vendor
- is devoted to her family
- dresses well. Filipinas strive to look clean and beautiful. They like modest but fashionable clothing. Skimpy blouses and mini-skirts are a 'no-no!' unless they are 'ladies of the night.'
- always has her umbrella. It shields her from the hot sun on dry days and keeps her dry on those unexpected rainy days. The Filipina and her umbrella are inseparable!
- doesn't smoke. Few Filipinas smoke. Smokers tend to be young women who want to look hip, just like their western celebrity idols in the movies or television. Smoking is considered cheap and very unlady-like.
- doesn't drink. While Filipino males are known to be gin and beer drinkers, Filipinas are not.
- does not initiate conversation

with men. Raised as demure and modest individuals, they wait for men to initiate a dance, a conversation, or an invitation to dinner.

- does not exhibit torrid acts of love in public. Filipinas are very sweet to their men, but they limit their public displays of affection to a peck on the cheek or holding hands.

Women

DO be wary of cab drivers. Women have fallen prey to taxi drivers who take advantage of their female passengers. Instead of delivering them to their destination, they are unwillingly brought to a dark area and raped. Always check the doors of cabs. Some taxis cannot be opened from inside, so the helpless passenger cannot easily escape. It's best not to take a cab alone at night. If you must, take a hotel cab. It's a more expensive but safer choice.

ZOOS, PARKS & MUSEUMS

Philippines

Public places like zoos, parks, and museums in the Philippines may not be as impressive as those in your home country. Nonetheless, you may learn a thing or two or may even be entertained. Support and respect these attractions. With your patronage, we hope they will see marked improvements.

DO lend this country a hand when visiting public places by not defacing, damaging, or destroying anything. While some parks and public places are not in the best shape, proper care and respect is still expected. Set a good example to locals by disposing of garbage in trashcans.

DO be more selective when buying food and drinks from vendors around recreation park boundaries. While the food is cheap and attractive, don't be enticed. These vendors have little water for washing and some may give you a stomach ache that could ruin your trip. Even locals refer to them as "dirty food".

DO say "no" to offers of stuffed animals or animal skin goods from shops or itinerant peddlers. Stuffed *tarsiers* (an endangered species of small monkey unique to the Philippines) and eagles must not be purchased. For those who love eating special delicacies like shark's fin, shark meat, bird's nest, and snake meat, STOP eating them. They may be delicious and provide you momentary enjoyment but think of the future of these animals. As long as people buy live or dead endangered wildlife, locals will continue selling them. If no one buys, the trade will end.

ZIGZAGS

Philippines

These last few titbits on Filipino culture will add to your pleasurable stay in our country. Besides being helpful, interesting or even entertaining, they may answer questions that you are shy to ask your Pinoy friends. The topics are not arranged in any particular order. It may zig from anything like the laundry and zag to something like bugs and later zig to cockfights and then zag to another topic.

Hopefully, you will find these zigzags helpful. Take it easy, Filipinos are generally laid back and informal. They easily forgive and forget mistakes.

What's in a name?

Filipinos' names are quite complex but often fascinating. An infant is usually baptised with several, some having six names on their certificate. Relatives are thrilled when a newborn child is named after them. A daughter is often named after her grandmother. Fathers are honoured by naming their children after them, followed by a Junior, III or IV after the name. Mr. Jose Santos may name his son Jose Santos, Jr. and his grandchild would likely be Jose Santos, III, and so on.

The Catholic faith influences the names of Filipinos. Our grandparents had biblical Spanish names like Concepcion (after the Immaculate Conception), Magdalena (after Mary Magdalene), Natividad (after the Nativity) and Jesus. While Filipinos still choose names from the saints, they don't sound as old fashioned anymore. Most names are still inspired by biblical characters and saints, but sound more contemporary like Regina, Teresa, Sarah, Ann, and Victoria for women and Martin, Joseph and Miguel for men. But the most popular name among women is Maria, Mary, or Marie, in honour of the Blessed Virgin.

Some parents are less creative, they settle for generic names like Boy, Girlie or Baby. Ask around, you will surely meet several Boy's, Girlie's and Baby's, even during a short visit. Even though it sounds awkward to be called Baby or Boy as a fifty-year-old adult, Filipinos seem to find nothing wrong with it. Recently, less cutesy American names like Catherine, Christine, Tanya, Carol, Karen, Julie, Patricia, John and Joey have become quite popular.

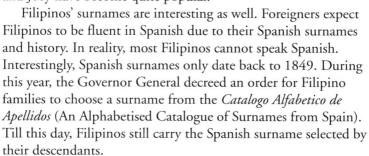

Filipinos' surnames are interesting as well. Foreigners expect Filipinos to be fluent in Spanish due to their Spanish surnames and history. In reality, most Filipinos cannot speak Spanish. Interestingly, Spanish surnames only date back to 1849. During this year, the Governor General decreed an order for Filipino families to choose a surname from the *Catalogo Alfabetico de Apellidos* (An Alphabetised Catalogue of Surnames from Spain). Till this day, Filipinos still carry the Spanish surname selected by their descendants.

Be aware that Filipinos refer to their mother's maiden name as their middle names. For example, Marga Reyes Guerrero, her middle name is Reyes, since her mother's unmarried name was Corazon Reyes.

Filipinos have many names, some even have five names. Oddly, some don't use their multiple names. Instead, friends, family and colleagues usually call them by their simple nicknames. A woman baptised as Maria Cristina Monica Ann Santos Pineda rarely uses any of those names. She prefers being called by her nickname, Tina. A shorter version of the name works well as a nickname. Juan Christian is called JC, Patricia becomes Patty, Yolanda answers to Yoly, Cory for Corazon. Some Filipinos take fancy in creating nicknames out of a repeated syllable of the first name like Tintin for Christine or Len-len for Arlene... Sometimes, parents choose flippant nicknames without any connection to actual names like Dingdong, Ruffles, Bubbles, Dimples, Cherry Pie or even Lucky.

DO address your business acquaintance by his or her family name such as "Ms. Pineda". Once you get comfortable with each other, she may ask you to call her by her first name or even by her nickname.

DO ask your aquaintances how they want to be called. There are no hard and fast rules, it's often simply a matter of preference. Former President Corazon Aquino did not mind being referred to as Cory most of the time.

Laundry

Clothes are usually hand washed by a *lavandera* (or laundry woman). She may stay with the family or come in daily, twice or thrice a week depending on their arrangement. She washes all clothes and linen by hand and irons them too.

In recent years, a number of laundromats have sprouted in the metropolis. These establishments offer complete laundry services from washing, drying and ironing

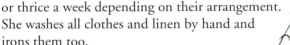

to dry cleaning. Most establishments charge by the kilo. You may ask the attendant to wash for you, or you may use their machines yourself. For dry cleaning you are charged per piece of clothing (this varies depending on the item). Some laundromats offer to pick up your dirty clothes and return them nice and clean, without any additional cost. They are a cheaper alternative to hotel laundry services. Check the local telephone directories for numbers.

Security guard

Security guards are men or women clad in a navy blue uniform, a badge, and equipped with a gun. Hotels have them stationed at their entrance, so do restaurants. Banks have three or four of them guarding the door with their long armalites. They are supposed to keep unwanted visitors and robbers away. They're everywhere - malls, discos, movie houses and posh villages. The number of security guards in Manila alone amazed an Australian visitor. He said, "There are so many of them, they can compete with the army." Well, he's probably right!

Basketball

Filipinos' favourite pastime is playing and watching basketball games. It comes as no surprise that the most popular basketball player was voted to the Senate, even if he had no previous experience in politics. Some basketball players without acting prowess have several films and TV shows to their credit. Anyone who can shoot hoops well is immediately admired by Filipino men, women, and kids. Almost every single boy regardless of his height desires to make it in the professional basketball league. Because of this addiction to the ballgame, you're bound to find a basketball court even in the most remote *barrio*.

DO join in if basketball is your thing. Everyone will be delighted to see you play.

Lihi

It is believed pregnant women have strong desires called *lihi* during their first trimester; desires which they cannot control. They take a fancy to anything from fruits to weird food combinations. Sour unripe green mangoes dipped in salty *bagoong* (shrimp paste) is a favourite. The suffering husband must move heaven and earth to satisfy his wife's cravings. If he fails, the mother and child become unhappy and difficulties may arise during the pregnancy. When the child is born, traits of the food craved for are evident in the physical characteristics of the infant. Indulging in chocolates will result in a dark child; white food like tofu will ensure a pale baby.

Some entertaining **DOs** and **DON'Ts** for Filipino pregnant women:

DON'T eat flukes of nature, like two connected bananas, if you are not too keen on giving birth to twins.

DON'T watch an eclipse, or you will give birth to a physically deformed child.

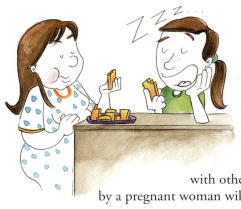

DON'T wear a scarf around your neck, as this may cause the child's death in the womb.

DON'T cut your hair or you will have a bald child.

DON'T share your food with other people. Eating food touched by a pregnant woman will cause you to become sleepy.

Sabong (Cockfight)

On every given day of the week throughout the year, in almost all parts of the country, hundreds of roosters are encouraged to fight. The *sabong* or cockfight is a popular betting game in the Philippines, especially among males. Spectators place a bet on one of the two cocks fighting. If his favoured cock wins, he wins a cash prize.

It is said there are two buildings you are sure to find in almost every town in the Philippines: a Church and a *sabungan* (or cockpit)!

Street rest rooms

For people who avoid losing face or *hiya*, visitors are perplexed to see men who are not at all embarrassed to pee in public in broad daylight. Filipino males have no qualms about relieving themselves on a wall along a busy street at any time of the day. Don't be shocked when your cab driver suddenly stops his car, gets out and turns the nearest wall into a urinal. There is a law against this antisocial

dos & don'ts **in the PHILIPPINES**

behaviour. It comes as no surprise that only a few are apprehended because the cops use the walls as a rest room, too.

Blame it on the inadequate number of toilets. But if that's the case, then women should be relieving themselves on the streets, too. Since they don't, it points to the Filipino males' lack of discipline and poor bladder control!

DON'T pee on walls or trees. Instead use the decent restrooms found in the malls, restaurants and hotels. Hold your bladder as long as you can, instead of turning the streets into one giant toilet.

Pasalubong

A long journey out of the country or a short trip out of town deserves a *pasalubong*. A *pasalubong* is the customary gift brought back to kin and friends from a trip. Usually, it's some speciality product the place is known for like peanut brittle from Baguio, pastillas from Bulacan, marble from Romblon, or even the aphrodisiac Durian from Davao. Be it a big or small *pasalubong*, it is the act of remembering the recipient that matters. This custom of bringing home *pasalubong* has caused Filipinos to bring home huge luggage or *balikbayan* boxes from their trips abroad. Filipinos have become famous (or rather infamous) in airports throughout the world for their overweight gigantic luggage.

DON'T forget to bring *pasalubong* for your close Filipino friends or to take some back for your loved ones.

Ningas kugon

Ningas Kugon is procrastination with a Pinoy twist. It is characterised by a shortlived enthusiasm for a certain endeavour, which is started with fanatical frenzy but ends in accomplishing nothing. This behaviour is prevalent in government organisations where what may appear as impressive projects never reach completion or are completed halfheartedly. Likened to *ningas kugon* or grassfire, the enthusiasm and commitment to an activity burn out quickly.

DON'T be fooled by the excitement at the start of a project. It could be purely *ningas kugon* at work. If you wish a project to reach completion, assume a leadership role, without being bossy. Filipinos get turned off by dominant bossy personalities. Instead, provide ample motivation to sustain the fire ignited at the beginning of a project. It's tricky, but don't let *ningas kugon* prevent you from completing your projects.

Faith healer

While many Filipinos employ Western medical practices to alleviate aches and pains, many (especially those in the province) prefer a faith healer to a doctor. Physical disorders are relieved through the person's belief in the power of divine intervention through direct prayer or the medication of the healer.

Some faith healers even claim to operate without using surgical instruments leaving no scars after the operation and attributing it to divine aid. Investigative journalists, dubbing it 'psychic surgery', discovered there was no operation to speak of. Quick movement of hands, a lot of acting and animals' blood were the ingredients of this spectacular but ultimately, mock surgery.

When western medicine failed them, some Americans and Europeans travelled to the Philippines to obtain help from traditional faith healers. Whether their therapies work or not is uncertain. But one thing is sure, millions of Filipinos in the *barrios* have never seen a physician in their lives relying instead on their trusted faith healer and herbal medicine.

DO seek the services of a physician when you get sick. If you are staying in a remote *barrio*, go to the nearby city. There will surely be a doctor and hospital there to help you out.

Palakasan

Palakasan is a scheming way of getting ahead through favours from others using one's connections with influential people. For example, the President of the country may grant your wish if you convey it through his friends. Being related to the head of the Land Transportation Office may help you get your driver's license faster. Sadly, there are two ways to succeed in this country: to work hard or to simply have the right connections in high places!

Mail

A local newspaper recently featured a postcard sent from the Philippines in 1956 which arrived at its US destination only in 1999. The good news is this is a rare case. Philippine mail may be slow, but it does not usually take this long. Local mail is delivered within three to five days, airmail at least ten days.

It is not advisable to mail cheques to and from the Philippines. If you must send a cheque, use reputable couriers like DHL and FedEx. Or you may opt to wire money through the bank with the corresponding service fee. For packages and important documents, a courier is also recommended. If you find it too costly, a cheaper but slower option is 'registered mail'.

DON'T look for mailboxes along the streets. You won't find any! This is because there are no postal vehicles to collect mail from the mailboxes. Take your letters, postcards, and packages to the post office. Check with the concierge of your hotel, if they can offer you a postal service.

E-mail

One of the greatest inventions of recent times is e-mail or electronic mail. There are a number of cybercafés in Metro Manila offering internet access at reasonable rates. Most hotels have business centres offering internet services too. E-mail allows you to keep in touch with relatives and friends back home at a fraction of the price of overseas calls and at a faster speed than regular mail.

Bakla

Gays or *baklas* are generally accepted in Filipino society. Many have carved a niche as couturiers, interior decorators, hair stylists, comedians and performers. So colourful and creative are they that *baklas* have their own lingo. Manila's nightlife also includes a number of clubs which feature gay entertainers. While many *baklas* openly express their femininity, not all gays exhibit this flamboyant behaviour.

First lady

The most infamous First Lady in the Philippines was Imelda Marcos and her thousands of pairs of shoes. However, she was not the only First Lady in the country. The President's wife is called the First Lady of the Philippines, the Mayor of Manila's wife is the First Lady of Manila, the wife of the Governor of Ilocos is the First Lady of Ilocos, and so on. Even before obtaining the title, the future first lady actively campaigns for her husband. She delights the voters by singing or dancing during campaign rallies. Many husbands and boyfriends of actresses have made it to Senate and Congress, thanks to their wives' enjoyable performances on the campaign trail. Once accorded the title as First Lady, she works on civic and tourism projects to benefit her husband's constituents. Recently, more and more women are elected to public office. The term 'First Gentleman' has come into popular use to describe Miguel Arroyo, the husband of President Gloria Arroyo. What good causes he will adopt or what his role will be apart from accompanying Mrs. President to balls and dinners, remains to be seen.

Miron

Be it a fist fight, a minor car accident, or a dangerous *coup d'etat*, you're sure to find spectators or *miron*. Whether the event is big or small, pleasant or unpleasant, the Filipino *miron* is there to witness it. Blame it on the curious nature of Pinoys, they always want to be part of the action. Or maybe it's the thrill of being able to boast later on, "I was there when it happened."

Friendly species

Just like other tropical islands, insects are abundant. There are over two thousand species sharing this archipelago with Filipinos. Two in particular deserve special mention because you're bound to come across them. There are the cockroaches or *ipis* who find their way into your house or room without any trouble; and the pale whitish grey small lizard or *butiki,* often called gekko, which clings to the walls and takes care of eating the mosquitoes. It also squeaks and clicks its tongue. Don't worry both are harmless.

One bug we hope you won't come across is the *surot* or bed bug that bite their helpless victim as he slumbers. You're more likely to find *surot* in the cheapest of hotels and hostels.

DO examine carefully all your clothes if you've been bitten by bed bugs. These tiny, resilient insects hide themselves in the seams and folds of your clothes and sleeping bag. Unfortunately for you, the most effective way of killing them is to squeeze them between your fingernails. It's a smelly and messy process.

DIs

For the past few years, ballroom dancing has become very popular in the Philippines. Society matrons hire the services of DIs or dance instructors to teach them the cha-cha, boogie, tango, flamenco. The DI is hired by the hour at the disco ballroom or for the whole evening. Private lessons may also be conducted in your own house. Some would like to impress friends with their dancing skills, so they bring their DIs along to parties. With all the evenings spent together dancing, many have had secret affairs with their dancing partners. Men have also caught ballroom fever. They have their own female DIs. So popular are DIs and ballroom dancing, even some public parks offer their services.

Classified posts?

"LOSE/GAIN 30 pounds?" call 724-3784, "PLUMBER call 810-1901", "Math Tutor call 811-2345"… No, these are not ads found in the classifieds of the newspapers. They are signs posted on lamp posts and electricity posts in the Philippines. The otherwise naked posts provide free advertising space for these enterprising business people. Some fast-food chains with delivery services post their ads there too. During election campaigns, 'poster anarchy' sets in with posters of all the candidates creating a messy collage on the poles.

The *Carabao*

You can't miss them. They're the greyish black water buffaloes at work in the rice fields. While modern farmers have tractors, most Filipino farmers have their trusted *carabao*. This beast is more than an agricultural machine. He's the farmer's best friend who helps plough the soil and carry the harvest. He also doubles as a means of transport for his boss. And in death, his meat is consumed in special dishes. Can a tractor do all that?

Videoke & Karaoke

Remember Imelda crooning to her husband Ferdinand in public? Well, all Filipinos love to sing. If you hand them a microphone, they may never stop. Karaoke and Videoke bars provide the perfect venue for wannabe singers. Karaoke bars offer singers with a microphone the chance to humiliate themselves in front of an audience. The videoke is more 'singer-friendly' as a television flashes the lyrics of the song, acting as a prompter for the amateur songbird. Fortunately, many Filipinos are blessed with good singing voices. There are also those who seem to be tone deaf, yet have no qualms about grabbing the mike to sing all night. After several bottles of beer has been consumed, the singing becomes bearable for other patrons in the bar!

To round up the whole idea

DO be alert, smart, and calm for anything and everything in the Philippines - anywhere, anytime. More often, it is NOT the Pinoy's fault. And if things go wrong, as they sometimes will, do as the Filipinos do - take it easy and SMILE!

DON'T be scared. Being in a foreign land, everything seems scary, strange, and unfamiliar. But this is the beauty of travelling. New experiences are fun, exciting, and oftentimes very enlightening when you keep an open mind. If you wish for what is familiar, then just stay at home.

Remember - no trip is perfect, each one has its difficulties and problems. But every journey makes you wiser!

And finally, to quote a reminder that provides good food for thought for all good visitors:

Take nothing but photographs.

Kill nothing but time.

Leave nothing but footprints.